THE BATTLE OF THE GRAVESTONES & THE SAYLESVILLE MASSACRE OF 1934

Patrick Crowley

CONTENTS

PREFACE

This work explores the history of events in Rhode Island connected to the 1934 General Textile Strike. During the strike, two people were killed by soldiers of the Rhode Island National Guard in an event known as "The Saylesville Massacre." The established historiography of the 1934 General Textile Strike does not tell the story of the Saylesville Massacre well. Despite claims to the contrary, the strike was poorly run and lost by the union. Through a careful reading of primary sources this work argues that only by understanding the 1934 General Textile Strike as a loss for the union can both Labor History and the Labor Movement learn from its example.

This short book, originally a master's thesis submitted and accepted by the University of Rhode Island, is the product of years of research that began with walks around the village of Saylesville in Lincoln, Rhode Island, where I live with my family. The hulking factory at the heart of the village was now home to a gym, a few art studios, and even a fencing academy. But at one time, it was the largest cotton bleachery in the world, and it just seemed like it had a story to tell.

Many thanks to the people who helped this project along the way, including Professors Erik Loomis and Miriam Reumann, Scott Molloy, Jay Walsh, and the members of the Rhode Island Labor History Society. This work would not have been possible with out the love and support of my wife Karen Bradbury.

INTRODUCTION

On September 1, 1934, the United Textile Workers of America (UTW) began a nationwide strike against the American cotton textile industry. More than 500,000 workers walked off the job, making the 22-day long strike one of the largest labor actions in American history. While national in scale the bulk of the workers impacted were in the American South, New England, Pennsylvania, and New Jersey.[1] During the strike in Rhode Island violent clashes between workers and security forces resulted in four deaths. In the small textile village of Saylesville, Rhode Island, confrontations between neighborhood residents, area workers, and security forces led to a week-long street battle resulting in dozens of arrests, the wounding of scores, and the deaths of two men - Charles Gorcynski and William Blackwood - in an incident known in Rhode Island labor lore as "The Saylesville Massacre."

The historiography of the 1934 textile workers strike includes references to the confrontations in Saylesville, particularly during the peak of the action between September 7 and September 12, but the Saylesville Massacre is not explored in great depth. Most scholars properly catalogue the incident as one of the most violent of the strike but because the Saylesville Massacre is one of many violent incidents in a national strike, not enough detail is provided to properly explain why Saylesville turned so viciously violent. This book seeks to remedy this historiographical gap. After introductory remarks providing historical background about the village of Saylesville and factory at the center of the story, this book will explore the national circumstances prompting the strike. The book will describe the union leading the strike along with the men leading the union. My attention will then shift towards the events of the strike in Rhode Island.

In a way it is understandable not much is known about the Saylesville Massacre. The key primary source about the strike in Rhode Island is the state's daily newspaper, *The Providence Journal*. The newspaper is known for its anti-union animus and during the strike its slanted coverage of the events is clear. But the newspaper's more direct impact on the record are the poorly written and badly edited stories about the strike. While it may be understandable a newspaper trying to publish up-to-the-minute accounts of the movements of thousands of people would sacrifice complete accuracy for the sake of current information, the newspapers stories written during the actual events are nearly incoherent. Stories beginning with the events of one day make unexplained, non-linear leaps to other days or other times within the same day. Researchers looking broadly at the events of the strike can be forgiven for not being able to put the pieces of the puzzle together.

Another reason for the lack of scholarly attention on the Saylesville Massacre could also be the lack of records with the union at the center of the story – the UTW. Textile unions never enjoyed significant density in Rhode Island and while the UTW claimed at the time of the strike to have over 50 local unions in the state, most of them appear to be very small. Also, in the years just after the strike, the UTW was torn apart in the battles between the American Federation of Labor and the newly formed Congress of Industrial Organizations. The small organization became smaller through civil war.

But these barriers are not the real reason why the Saylesville Massacre is nearly forgotten and misremembered in labor history. My thesis is the strike in Rhode Island was disorganized and poorly run and directly contributed to the deaths in the Saylesville Massacre. The year 1934 saw several massive strikes around the country, many of them resulting in significant victories for the working class, but the national textile strike was lost by the union and its members. In Rhode Island, the strike was an embarrassment to the labor movement and to Governor Theodore Francis

"TF" Green, a Democrat and supporter of the New Deal. For both the labor movement and the governor to continue their path to political power in the state, the facts of the textile strike and the events in Saylesville needed to be swept aside; so, they were.

This book presents three arguments. First, the established historiography has not told the story of the Saylesville Massacre or the events of 1934 textile strike in Rhode Island particularly well. By accepting the union's declaration of victory at the conclusion of the strike scholars have ignored some obvious facts about the union's ineffective conduct of the strike. The UTW was woefully unprepared to engage in a strike of this magnitude. They had neither the staff nor the financial resources to confront a complicated industry on a national scale. The union's track record in major confrontations was abysmal and they did not demonstrate any meaningful steps to prepare for the national strike. Despite claims by some that the union was well organized in Rhode Island, I will show that it was not. The disorganization contributed to the tragedy on the streets of Saylesville.

Secondly, the strike was a loss, and Labor History as a discipline should approach the subject from that perspective. Scholars like John Salmond, Janet Irons and Cletus Daniel, discussed below, do an admirable job of explaining the deficits of the UTW, but more research is required to understand the impact of the loss of the strike. One area for future scholars to consider is how the defeat of the textile strike impacted southern workers attitudes towards unionizing for generations to come. Did the failure of the union to adequately support the striking workers contribute to the failure of subsequent organizing efforts in the South? Yes is a reasonable answer but to explore this hypothesis, one must first approach the strike as lost by the union. That means challenging the union's claims which, at least in the Rhode Island context, I do below.

Finally, it is important for the labor movement to accept the 1934 textile strike as a loss to learn from its mistakes. The historiography of 1934 details a huge upswing in working-class activism, the roots of which are explored below. However, given the union organizing victories of that year, it is tempting to either shunt aside the details of the textile strike and the ineptitude of the union leading it, or worse, drift into hagiography about the year "labor erupted."   Leading working women and men out of their workplace and onto the picket lines is potentially putting workers in harm's way. It is not a decision to be taken lightly and holding up the Saylesville Massacre as a cautionary tale can help instruct union organizers on factors they need to take into consideration before launching a strike. Perhaps the primary factory for consideration when calling a strike is the strength of the union as an organization, not just as an idea. Strikes, and standing up to the boss, the cops, and the military can be thrilling and a great way to build working class solidarity...until the shooting starts.

The UTW never should have called the national textile strike of 1934. They were bullied into the action by a rank-and-file justifiably angry at their mistreatment in the workplace but who did not adequately appreciate the task before them. The Union knew they were not ready, but they forged ahead anyway, and in Saylesville, two workers were killed as a result. The UTW members, most of whom joined the union only months before the strike was announced, also bear some responsibility for the strike's failure. Not because they lacked resolve or a sense of solidarity - both were clearly on display - but because no matter how strong one's sense of union comradeship is felt, it will not stop the effects of tear gas in the lungs or bullet wounds to the head.

BACKGROUND

Saylesville is one of hundreds of former mill villages dotting industrial New England. Nestled in between Rhode Island rural highway routes 122 and 126, the village is one of the six in the town of Lincoln, five miles north of Providence, and bordering the city of Central Falls.[2] Originally known as "World's End," the village officially became Saylesville in 1881 when Samuel Fessenden was assigned postmaster to the newly opened post office to serve the community of workers and managers of the expanding bleachery business of brothers William F. and Frederick C. Sayles. By the time of the naming of Saylesville, the *W.F. & F.C. Sayles Co.* was the largest bleachery company in the world.[3]

In 1934, the bleachery at the heart of the village was called the Sayles Finishing Plant. At the time, bleacheries were a crucial link in the textile industry supply chain, processing raw cotton to make it clean and white. Bleaching textiles in the early twentieth century was still an ancient, somewhat occult, trade. One writer describes the process as 'surrounded by such an aura of mystery' with routines passed from father to son like secret recipes.[4] Made modern in the eighteenth century with the introduction of chemicals such as chlorine, the process retained many ancient characteristics. For example, a critical step in the process is known as 'souring.' In the early twentieth century souring involved treating boiled cotton with a chlorine-based mixture known as 'chemic' but in earlier times "souring" was accomplished by washing boiled cotton through buttermilk.[5] It is easy to imagine the inside of the bleachery looking like an industrial scale mad scientist laboratory complete with bubbling cauldrons, jets of water and steam, chutes, box folders, and dripping, stinking rolls of cotton hanging from rafters above the heads of workers using large wooden sticks to stir treated fabric through caustic pots of soapy solution. The odors of sugar, chlorine, and burnt vegetables waft through the air, letting everyone in the factory, and the surrounding neighborhood, know exactly what step of the process was underway.[6]

Working at the bleachery was tough, smelly labor and tensions periodically boiled over into conflict. In the fall of 1905, the Saylesville workers went on strike for better pay. The strike began in the folding room of the plant after workers, paid $10 per week, demanded a ten-percent pay increase. The workers were angry with the company for hiring Henry Laurence Gantt, an expert in so-called Scientific Management. Gantt was recommended to bleachery management by Frederick Taylor, the founder of Scientific Management as someone who could transform Sayles' company from a collection of foreman-led fiefdoms into a modern enterprise. According to Gantt's biographer L.P. Alford, the workers chafed at Gantt's methods and in late October, 1905, the rise in tensions prompted a walkout.[7] Strikes against Scientific Management were common in the early twentieth century, as Hugh Aitken points out in *Scientific Management in Action: Taylorism at Watertown Arsenal, 1908-1915* about a similar strike in 1911, in Watertown, Massachusetts.[8] A 1905 trade publication, *American Wool & Cotton Reporter*, wrote that after several weeks of the strike the workers "profess to have no fear of the results" and on November 17, *The Boston Daily Globe* reported the workers won their all of their demands, including a reduction from 60 to 58 weekly working hours without loss of pay.[9]

Seventeen years later a statewide strike of Rhode Island textile factory hands started when factory owners announced a statewide 20-percent wage cut. Area textile workers, mostly without formal union support, spontaneously abandoned their looms and walked off the job. On February 4, over a thousand workers marched three miles from the neighboring city of Pawtucket to Saylesville, hoping to parade in front of the bleachery. Several inches of freshly fallen snow did not stop the marchers, but reports vary about their reception when they arrived in Saylesville. Susan Jaffee tells us in her master's thesis "Ethnic Working Class Protest: The Textile Strike of 1922 in Rhode Island" how local media reported one hundred of the Saylesville workers joined the pickets while the UTW, which had a small loom fixers local at the plant, claimed 500-600 workers joined in.[10] Despite the divergent numbers, at least for a time the bleachery was closed.

The national conditions leading up to the textile strike of 1934 are extensively discussed in scholarly works like *The Turbulent Years: A History of the American Worker, 1933-1940,* by Irving Bernstein; *Testing the New Deal: The General Textile Strike of 1934 in the American South,* by Janet Irons; *Culture of Misfortune: An Interpretive History of Textile Unionism in the United States* by Cletus Daniel, and *The General Textile Strike of 1934: From Maine to Alabama,* by John Salmond.[11] The consensus in the literature about the national textile strike of 1934 is the hopes of workers to find relief from the depravations of the Great Depression by organizing unions, as envisioned in the National Industrial Recovery Act of 1933 were dashed by stiff employer opposition. Only a strike on a national scale could possible address this injustice.

A key provision of the National Industrial Recovery Act was Section 7(a), which for the first time in American legislative history gave the federal government's legal support to union organizing. The section read in part:

...employees shall have the right to organize and bargain collectively through representatives of their own choosing, and shall be free from interference, restraint, or coercion of employers of labor, or their agents, in the designation of such representatives or in the self-organization or in other concerted activities for the purpose of collective bargaining or other mutual aid or protection.[12]

However, even though Section 7(a) played a role in sparking workers' interests in union organizing, the law was quickly viewed by workers as a 'broken promise' given how hard employers fought back against union organizing efforts. As a result, Bernstein tells us, "In 1934, labor erupted." The year was marked by over 1,800 strikes involving almost a million and a half workers across the country.[13]

The Turbulent Years is a long and comprehensive review of the ebbs and flows of worker organizing during the first eight years following the initial inauguration of Franklin Delano Roosevelt as President of the United States on March 4, 1933. The book offers a comprehensive review of the other key strikes of 1934, including the Toledo Auto-Lite strike, the Minneapolis Teamster strike, and the West Coast Longshoremen strikes. He rightly includes the national textile strike led by the UTW as one of the key events in this year of heavy strike activity, explaining the strike was prompted by textile manufacturers deliberately undermining the spirit and intent of Section 7(a).

Interestingly, Daniel's *Culture of Misfortune* claims that while Section 7(a) was indeed a turning point for organized labor's ambitions to organize on a large scale, it was considered a throwaway, last minute addition to the bill during drafting and the legislation's sponsors did not conceive it would lead to massive organizing of the depression era proletariat.[14] Daniel's book discusses elements of the 1934 strike, but its major subject is the UTW itself, an organization he describes as having an "unfortunate genius for self-destruction." Daniel's comprehensive understanding of the UTW is critical to explaining their role in leading the textile strike, especially their "Ox-cart tactics in an automobile age."[15] It is a point seconded by Richard Kelly in his book *Nine Lives For Labor* where he characterizes the UTW as "born in debt and died in bankruptcy."[16]

Irons' *Testing the New Deal* takes an equally dim view of the UTW. Her book documents the various factions tugging at the union and its leadership, but critically, locates the national strike in the context of a northern based union with an increasingly large and restive southern membership. Meticulously documented and supplemented with personal interviews of southern strike survivors, Irons' work focuses specifically on the southern worker experience of the New Deal through the activity of the national textile strike. In this way, her book is similar to Lizabeth Cohen's *Making a New Deal: Industrial Workers in Chicago, 1919-1939* and Elizabeth Faue's *Community of Suffering & Struggle: Women, Men, and the Labor Movement in Minneapolis, 1915-1945*, both of which study the lived experience of the working class in a particular geographic area during the New Deal era.[17] For Irons, "How southern textile workers mobilized in response to the New Deal is key to explaining the passion of the '34 strike."[18]

The strikes of 1934, while thoroughly documented in the historiography, because of their mostly triumphant results, are susceptible to hagiography. For the general textile strike, what my analysis shows is in addition to any weaknesses in the law and its enforcement, the UTW was in no place to be able to lead a strike on a national scale. Structurally and financially the union did not have the resources nor staff to pull off an action of this size, but they tried anyway, and the results were disastrous. While scholars like Daniel and Irons do point to the weakness of the UTW, the culpability for the strike's failure has not sufficiently been explored. In part what I attempt to do below is build on the work of Daniel and Irons and through the example of Saylesville, make a connection for the strike's failure directly to the union.

PRELUDE TO THE GENERAL TEXTILE STRIKE

United Textile Workers President Thomas McMahon and Vice President Francis Gorman were both Rhode Islanders. Thomas McMahon was in his mid-sixties at the time of the strike (he was never sure if he was born in 1870 or 1868). He emigrated from Ireland as a boy to Rhode Island and worked in textile mills throughout the state. McMahon joined the Knights of Labors but after the order faded away he joined the UTW, three years after the union's founding in 1901. Active in the union from the day he joined, he worked his way up the leadership ranks, joining the national executive board in 1906, eventually rising to the presidency in 1921.[19]

Francis Gorman was about a decade younger than McMahon, emigrating from England to Rhode Island at the age of 13. He too worked in mills across Rhode Island before becoming an organizer for the UTW. He was elected national Vice President in 1928, assigned to the role of lead organizer for the UTW's southern organizing campaign. The campaign, which the UTW under-resourced financially and understaffed with experienced organizers, ended in disaster, with several strikes crushed by the National Guard.[20] Janet Irons points out Gorman was not only frustrated by the power of the southern mill owners, but also with the 'indifference' the UTW displayed toward organizing the southern millworkers into the union.[21]

With Gorman's failure to organize the southern mill

workers, the UTW languished as the depression grew deeper. Its national membership hovered around 15,000 and it once more teetered on the brink of economic collapse.[22] But in 1932, with the election of Franklin D. Roosevelt, and the passage of the NIRA, the UTW was offered a lifeline. The passage of the NIRA created the National Recovery Administration (NRA) and gave the federal government significant oversight in core American industries hit hard by the Depression, including textiles. The NIRA suspended antitrust laws for a period of two years, gave the NRA the ability to set codes of fair competition within industries, establish minimum wages, and set maximum hours. One of the first industries to establish a code was textiles.

Even before Congress finalized the NIRA, the Cotton Textile Institute (CTI), headed by George Sloan, began drafting language for a "Code of Fair Competition." The CTI began in 1926 as a voluntary association of textile manufactures attempting to self-regulate the industry. The organization tried to get the industry to agree to voluntary production quotas to head off repeated cases of over production which plagued textile manufacturing for decades. By 1932, CTI was recognized as the official spokes group for the industry, but early in 1933, Sloan concluded without government intervention, the industry was too competitive to agree to voluntary self-regulation.[23]

Within a month of the signing of the NIRA, the textile industry presented to General Hugh Johnson, the director of the NRA, a draft code of competition.[24] In a nod to liberals in the New Deal Administration, the code banned child labor, long a scourge of textile manufacturing.[25] The code also, despite the industry's public opposition to unions and collective bargaining, included the organizing rights supposedly guaranteed under Section 7(a). The code established a two-tier wage system for textile workers - $12/week for companies operating in the South and $13/week for those in the North. It also restricted production to two, forty-hour shifts per week and a maximum work week of forty-hours per worker. The textile industry code was the first approved by the NRA and both industry and labor leaders praised the code as a model of cooperation and some workers declared it represented their "industrial declaration of independence. [26]

General Johnson named George Sloan as the government's representative and chair of the textile industry code board. As Sloan began working on implementation, concerns surfaced because the code made no mention of the 'stretch-out.' For decades, when textile production needs increased, or if manufacturers wanted to squeeze more profits out of their labor, they increased the workload of mill hands. While numbers varied from plant-to-plant, a 'stretch-out' required a worker originally assigned to tend five looms to be assigned to ten, possibly more. Not only did the stretch-out make the work of tending to large, noisy, machines more stressful and dangerous, it meant the manufacturer would need fewer workers.

When the original NIRA was under consideration, South Carolina Congressman John Clarence Taylor, himself a former textile worker, proposed an amendment prohibiting the use of the stretch-out in textile manufacturing. His amendment passed the House of Representatives but was removed from the final legislation in the conference committee with the Senate. To placate Taylor, General Johnson suggested modifying the code, after implementation, to prohibit the stretch-out. The modification, known as Section 15, proposed "no employee of any mill in the cotton textile industry shall be required to do any work in excess of practices…prevailing on July 1, 1933, unless such increase is submitted to an approved by the [new cotton textile industry committee] and by the National Recovery Administration." However, Sloan prevailed upon Johnston to delay implementation of Section 15 until the concerns giving rise to were properly studied, and Johnson agreed. Janet Irons astutely observes the "debate over Section 15 contained the seeds of a larger conflict."[27]

Johnson created a three-person panel to investigate the stretch-out known as the Cotton Textile National Industrial Relations Board (CTNIRB) and appointed an industry linked economist named Robert Bruere its chairperson. The other two people on the board were an anti-union manufacturer named Benjamin Geer from South Carolina and George Berry, president of the Printing Pressmen's union from Tennessee. Berry's appointment was hardly a victory for textile unions - he was known as a conservative labor leader who had openly criticized the UTW and textile workers for their propensity to strike and was skeptical over stretch-out concerns.[28]

It is important to understand what General Johnson allowed to happen in the textile industry. He adopted the code of competition crafted by the industry and then appointed the head of an industry group to oversee the code's enforcement. He created a three-person committee to investigate the most serious issue left unresolved by the code and then stacked the committee with appointees known to be sympathetic to the concerns of manufacturers. The UTW exerted little influence on the code or its implementation, and even when they tried, they chose to focus wage and hour issues, not the stretch-out.[29]

With the implementation of the code, Sloan predicted an immediate increase in employment. By September of 1933, he was able to report employment levels had grown by 150,000. In retrospect, the increased employment seems less connected to the code itself than a boost in production in anticipation of the implementation of new taxes on raw materials, including cotton, set to take place in October of 1933 thanks to the Agricultural Adjustment Act.[30] Described as a 'boomlet' by Irving Bernstein, the increased production was stealing "production and employment from the future."[31] Additionally, Janet Irons contends Sloan's committee started counting employment statistics months before the code was actually implemented, questioning the validity of attributing increased employment to the code.[32]

A rapid increase of membership in the UTW also began in 1933 after the adoption of the code. In early1933, the UTW was paying per capita tax to the AFL on only 15,000 members.[33] By September 1933, membership was at 40,000 and by June of 1934 they counted 250,000 members.[34] The largest increase was in the South, where local unions seemingly sprang up overnight; so much so that it was hard for the UTW to keep pace with demand.

Daniel quotes one UTW organizer in the saying "the initial fear of the worker to defy his boss has been to a certain degree allayed by this very official-looking pronouncement."[35] In both South and North Carolina there were enough newly formed local unions that workers could form central labor councils to coordinate activities. The same was true in Alabama, where six separate locals were formed in Walker County and more than 2,600 members joined a UTW local in Huntsville.[36]

After an initial surge in post-code employment, when the boomlet in production ended, demand dropped, and prices fell. However, production costs enforced by the code remained intact, and as a result, employment levels increased more than 12% and the stretch-out returned to mills, crushing workers with the increased workload. As thousands of workers were let go at plants around the country, those that remained were expected to do in eight hours what previously took twelve. "The jobs are just so bad stretched out," said one distressed worker. [37].

All worker complaints about job losses and the stretch were referred to the CTNIRB, which defended the interests of the industry and did next to nothing. Even if they had wanted to, the CTNIRB never had enough staff and resources to investigate the claims flooding into the agency. For example, of over 1700 wage and hour claims, only 96 were even investigated. Section 7(a) complaints about unlawful employer interference with union organizing, went unanswered or denied, giving employers a clear signal, they could ignore workers' collective bargaining rights with impunity. Adding insult to injury, the CTNIRB concluded its investigation of the stretch-out and concluded the practice was "sound in principle" if poorly implemented in some cases. Rather than enact General Johnson's proposed Section 15, Bruere's committee recommended a new Section 17, creating a system of mediation for complaints of overwork in the stretch-out. Of course, those complaints would be referred to the CTNIRB for mediation, ensuring they would die in the industry dominated committee.[38]

Adding to growing worker dissatisfaction with the NRA and the code, in May of 1934, Johnson authorized a reduction in work hours from 40 to 30 per week without increasing compensation making workers whole. Finally, the reticent if not docile UTW, spurred on by an angry and restless membership, told Johnson unless the decision was reversed, it would call a national strike. "There won't be a cotton mill open in the country in two weeks if this order is carried out," said the UTW's Francis Gorman.[39] The industry did not take Gorman's threat seriously. George Sloan challenged how many members were paying dues to UTW, telling Bruere to request an audit of the UTW's member books, saying "I'll bet they don't have 70,000 paid-up members." But when Bruere conducted the audit of the UTW membership numbers, he discovered the union had grown to over 270,000 members.[40] Despite its growing strength, the UTW blinked. After a two-day conference in early June, the UTW withdrew its strike demand in exchange for an additional representative on the CTNIRB. The textile industry cheered the result, calling a great victory for the bosses and defeat for the meddlesome union. To twist the knife even further, Sloan convinced Johnson to add an additional management representative to the board for 'balance.'[41]

The union members, particularly in the south, were furious the UTW acquiesced so quickly. On July 16, 1934, 20,000 workers in Huntsville, Alabama, walked off the job without sanction from the union, shutting 24 mills.[42] One worker told local press UTW President Thomas McMahon had killed the June strike, and "we're not going to let him kill this one."[43]

With a rank-and-file revolt on their hands, the UTW called an emergency executive board meeting on July 18 and decided to hold a national convention in New York City on August 13. At the convention, fifty separate resolutions calling for a national strike were introduced. One bandaged striking Huntsville, Alabama worker, Monroe Addock, took the convention floor and harangued the UTW leadership saying " I've been wounded in the head and shot in the leg, but I am willing to shed my blood again against the capitalists" to the roar of applause from the floor.[44] Socialist Party Leader Norman Thomas told the assembled delegates theirs was a "fight for justice" and described General Johnson as "the biggest noise with the least results of any man I ever heard."[45] When Tom McMahon addressed the members, he told them, "We are not desirous of creating chaos. I would hate to give my consent to anything like that (a national strike) unless I was absolutely convinced that it was the only way out. There is no other way. We will say to the manufacturers: now that we know the powers we possess, we will wield it, but we will wied (sic) it intelligently and reasonably."[46]

The convention faced other internal discord. McMahon was forced to tell delegates the UTW did not have sufficient funds to send any money to any of the local unions, but regardless of the union's precarious finances, the convention voted down a resolution to standardize dues across the country at $1 per member per month. Also, McMahon faced a leadership challenge from Emil Rieve of Milwaukee, Wisconsin. Ironically, Rieve was one of the few voices in the room to urge caution on the proposed strike authorization resolution. He told the crowd "we ought to bite off just as much as we can chew and not be swayed by the enthusiasm for a general strike."[47] Despite Rieve's warning, the UTW members voted overwhelmingly to strike - 561 in favor, 10 opposed.[48] McMahon also persuaded Rieve to drop his leadership challenge and the convention then re-elected McMahon and his team by acclamation.[49]

The convention also voted to give the executive committee the authority to set the strike date but instructed them to only give 12 hours' notice prior to the strike commencing.[50] McMahon appointed UTW Vice President Francis Gorman, chairperson of the strike committee. As the convention ended, Gorman laid out the demands of the coming strike: Better enforcement of the NRA code, especially around the payment of wages; an 'adjustment' to the stretch out; an end to discrimination against union members, and a 30-hour work week for 40 hours pay.[51]

After the UTW convention in August 1934 formally sanctioned the national strike, Gorman appointed another Rhode Islander, Joseph Sylvia, to lead the strike committee in New England

and Sylvia chose his home state for the base of operations. There is not much about Sylvia in the record, apart from a few mentions in literature from the TWUA-CIO, a separate union from the UTW formed during the years after the Congress of Industrial Organizations (CIO) split from the AFL. Sylvia stayed loyal to the AFL after the split, and when the two unions competed for members, TWUA-CIO literature referred to Sylvia as a "Little Caesar."[52]

Sylvia set up strike headquarters at the Labor Temple on 70 East Avenue in Pawtucket and began to assemble his team.[53] He appointed local UTW leaders Elizabeth Nord and Joseph Gray to coordinate activities in the southern part of the state and tasked Stella Moskwa and William Clark to cover the northern part.[54] Sylvia called for a meeting of all fifty-two Rhode Island UTW locals on Saturday, August 25th, at the larger Eagles Hall located on Snow Street in Providence.

While Sylvia jumped into action, local employers seemed nonplussed about the possibility of a strike. When asked about the strike, employers told one local newspaper that they were 'far from alarmed." "In fact," one boss told a reporter, "many of us would be glad to close our mill and let labor leaders bring about a situation which they cannot control." While some employers did not want their sentiments attributed to them, it is clear at this early stage that a communication pattern was emerging from the employer side. Coordinated or not, employers were, or at least wanted to be perceived as, unworried about the possibility of large-scale disruptions. "Most of our mills were operating at only 40 percent of their capacity," an employer noted, adding, "and that few of them had large orders ahead."[55]

At national UTW headquarters in Washington, D.C., union officials prepared for the looming strike. Speaking to a gathering of UTW leaders, Gorman gave instructions for how picket lines were to be conducted. He told the workers "be orderly, and remain orderly, always." Interestingly, he added, "Particularly be aware of communist intrigue. Keep your ranks free of communism and communist trickery. Stamp it out wherever it raises its head. Be stern about this."[56] He also said, "We will have to fight not only the employers and their hired thugs but the communists who are now trying to take advantage of this situation to promote their own philosophy."[57]

The UTW, like many of the unions affiliated with the American Federation of Labor (AFL), took strongly anti-communist positions in the early twentieth century. Cletus Daniel notes this was a specific strategy, aimed at portraying the AFL unions as a 'lesser of two evils," and thus attracting employer and public support, first when the International Workers of the World emerged as a competitor for the loyalties of the working class, and then later as the American Communist Party fought for workers' sympathy and allegiance. This strategy rarely worked, Daniel points out, but the UTW stuck to the play for decades.[58] In her book, *Common Sense Anti-Communism*, Jennifer Luff makes clear that the UTW was one of the more aggressively anti-communist unions, "vigorously" fighting Communist Party affiliated unions over jurisdiction representing textile workers.[59] In Rhode Island, the UTW was regularly challenged for union membership by the Communist Party affiliated National Textile Workers Union.

The American Communist Party answered Gorman's complaints against them in a series of articles published in *The Daily Worker* that were quickly converted into a pamphlet titled "Communists in the Textile Strike: An Answer to Gorman, Green and Co." [60] The breathlessly worded pamphlet seemed particularly concerned Gorman would sell out the strikers at the first opportunity and allow the dispute to be arbitrated rather than fought out in the streets. "Don't let Gorman, McMahon, or other A.F. of L. officials mislead you into accepting any treacherous arbitration scheme. Close down the mills and keep them closed with powerful mass picket lines."[61]

UTW leaders gathered at the union's Washington headquarters on August 30 to finalize their strike plans. McMahon and Gorman were joined by a delegation of other union leaders who travelled over from the AFL headquarters along with a gaggle of reporters. The normally affable UTW leaders were reportedly agitated and tense.[62] With the crowd hovering over the telegraph machine, Gorman sent the following telegram:

To all local unions, greetings. Strike of all cotton textile workers will begin at 11:30 O'clock, your time, Saturday night. Put all previous instructions into effect. Wool, silk, rayon and synthetic yarn membership stand by for further orders. Victory through solidarity.[63]

Gorman tried to read the telegram to the group but was drowned out by the cheers of the union leaders in the room. When the din subsided, Gorman issued the following statement to the press:

This telegram will call half a million workers to the strike lines. Not all of those are now employed. The stretch out which adds to the machine load of the worker until he can bear no more, has robbed thousands of these their chance to work. But every man and woman will rally to the strike lines and the great cotton textile industry will not move a wheel or thread after the hour set to stop the mills.[64]

The telegram was sent despite last minute efforts by Lloyd Garrison, head of the National Labor Relations Board, to avert a strike.[65] Throughout the day, Garrison conferred with UTW leaders and separately with George Sloan, the lead representative of the textile employers. The UTW appeared willing to conference with industry leaders and Garrison but Sloan refused to meet with the union representatives. Despite his reluctance to meet, Sloan told reporters, "I suppose every citizen in America is hopeful the strike won't take place."[66]

Despite the jubilant atmosphere, confusion set in at UTW headquarters. Regardless of the telegram's announcement of the strike start time, most locals were separately instructed to strike on Tuesday, September 4, the day after Labor Day. Regardless of that amendment to the instructions, some locals started their strike as soon as the news of the strike reached them. In Macron, Georgia, for example, workers at the Bibb Manufacturing plant walked off their jobs upon receipt of the telegram despite the threat issued by the company supervisor that "you automatically forfeit your positions."[67]

In Rhode Island, mill hands shared general excitement about the pending strike. The meeting on August 25 called by Sylvia was filled to capacity, and not only did delegates from all fifty-two Rhode Island locals attend, but the workers marched in a parade to the meeting from the Loom Fixers Union hall in the Olneyville section of Providence, down Westminster Street, to Eagles Hall. Reporters huddled outside the meeting, waiting for any news about the strike. When the meeting ended, the press reported the Rhode Island strike committee changed the time of the start of the strike from September 1 (a Saturday when the mills were closed) to September 4 (the day after the long holiday weekend), which Sylvia flatly denied.[68] Adding to the confusion, Sylvia was in a car accident the night of August 28. He crashed his car while trying to pass another driver on his way home to Barrington, Rhode Island, flipping it over and hitting a telephone pole. He broke his right wrist in the crash but survived.[69]

Sylvia's organizers met again at 2:00 Saturday afternoon, September 1, to make final strike preparations. Looking to clarify when the strike would take place, Sylvia walked back his earlier statements to the press and told reporters "we will picket every mill whose operatives have been called out, whether union or not" starting on Tuesday, September 4.[70] He also made clear the strike would be extended to the entire cotton industry, including workers in the worsted wool, silk, rayon, bleaching and dyeing, and printing industries. Sylvia made a point of singling out the bleaching industry, saying that bleachery workers "have been misled in many instances by the employers who infer that the strike does not apply to them and are also included in the strike order. Workers have been advised to take their place in the situation in order to correct once and for all the deplorable conditions under which these employees have been forced to work."[71] Rhode Island AFL Vice President Joseph Cahir also attended the gathering and told reporters the union coalition pledged "complete moral and financial support of the strike."[72] It was also announced that UTW President McMahon would be the guest of honor at the Rhode Island Labor Day parade scheduled for Monday in Providence.

Once again, mill owners shrugged off the threat of the strike. "We shall not pay any attention to the strike order whatsoever. The mill will be open Tuesday morning as usual," said Austin T. Levy, treasurer of the Stillwater Worsted Mill.[73] Joseph Cull, president of the Cull Silk Mill, said "in my candid opinion, the vast majority of silk workers don't want this strike, and as far as Rhode Island is concerned, this is a sympathy strike."[74] "The mill will remain open as usual on Tuesday morning as far as we know. We have not received any notice of this strike from our employes (sic). Some of our employes (sic), but by no means all, belong to the United Textile Workers," said Everett Salisbury, manager of the large Atlantic Mills in Providence.[75] "If the majority want to work we will give them employment. We have no issue with our employees," said R.H.L. Goddard, president of the Lonsdale Company.[76]

Despite the local mill owner reaction, nationally, textile operators were starting to ramp up their rhetoric. George Sloan told reporters:

"We cannot accept as justified the violent procedure of the strike against a Government code. We contend that the New Deal meant to offer a guarantee of liberty to employes (sic) - a real freedom of choice in their relationship to their employers. The American State cannot permit a majority of American men and women to be coerced into an organization to whose leadership they have not given their allegiance to whose financial support they do not desire to contribute.[77]

Confusing things further, a Rhode Island based independent union, the Independent Textile Union (ITU) of Woonsocket, raised doubts about participating in the strike. In *Working-Class Americanism: The Politics of Labor in a Textile City, 1914-1960*, historian Gary Gerstle reports the ITU initially voted against joining the strike. According to Gerstle, the ITU "did not share the grievances of workers elsewhere" because they had collective bargaining agreements in place that provided terms well above what was called for in the NIRA.[78] ITU Local President Joseph Schmetz told *The Providence Journal* that his members would only be "standing by" when the strike starts and told his members to report to work as scheduled on Tuesday.[79] Regardless of the status of the ITU's collective bargaining agreements, the union's reluctance to get involved, at least initially, could be understood in the context of their culturally different, and isolated, French-Canadian membership base.

On Monday, September 3, 10,000 people attended the annual Providence Labor Day parade. Four thousand union members, led by grand marshal Joseph Cahir, marched through the streets of Providence, accompanied by five marching bands. The largest single group of marchers were from the UTW, with 500 members in the parade. The parade passed a reviewing stand where UTW leaders McMahon and Sylvia were joined by Providence Mayor James Dunne, Newport Mayor Mortimer Sullivan, the Rev. Paul McElroy and several other local dignitaries. U.S. Congressman Francis Condon addressed the crowd, as did Rhode Island Socialist Party leader Joseph Coldwell.[80]

The highlight of the speaking program was UTW President McMahon. He told the crowd that when the strike begins, do not to turn the other cheek:

Hit back if you are hit. Fight back even if you are shot down... No man observes law and order more than I do, but if you're hit, hit back as hard as you can. Suffer, if you have to, and fight back, for that is the only way to gain freedom. I have no fight with the constituted authority of this State, but I know President Roosevelt would rather see mill workers fight for the justice he demands for all labor. No power on earth can stop it now. The cotton manufacturers said No, North and South, they are united for exploitation. All right, let it be a show-down. [81]

Seemingly trying to reassure the workers the UTW was ready for action, McMahon concluded his speech with "In spite of hell or high water we are going through with this strike."[82]

The drama of the day was not confined to the marching and the speeches. Just after Congressman Condon spoke, the Providence police arrested two men, Lawrence Spitz and Walter Petraska, who they accused of trying to disrupt the crowd. Spitz and Petraska were spotted throwing "showers of communist handbills" into the crowd, calling for the workers to engage in a general strike in support of the textile workers. The leaflets accused McMahon and Gorman of getting ready to "sell out" the strikers and demanded that the Communist Party affiliated National Textile Workers Union be included in the strike preparations. It would not be the last time that Spitz was apprehended by authorities during the strike.[83]

THE STRIKE BEGINS IN RHODE ISLAND

After the initial confusion about its official start time, the strike in Rhode Island started on Tuesday, September 4. The first days of the strike passed without major incident in the state. However, in other parts of the country, picket line violence immediately flared up; so local officials began to make preparations in case the same thing happened here. Rhode Island Governor Theodore Francis Green addressed the state's American Legion convention in Westerly, Rhode Island, on September 6, telling the Legionnaires:

"At such a time it is easy for passions to be aroused and when passions are aroused acts of violence are apt to occur. It behooves all citizens, not only those directly involved in the strike, but those indirectly affected by it, and that means all of us, to do our best to remain calm ourselves and to persuade others to be calm even in the face of provocation."[84]

The state's Attorney General, John Hartigan, a former commander of the Legion, told the crowd the forces of law and order were prepared for any eventuality and that "mob rule would not be tolerated in this state." [85]

The rest of the state's political establishment began to jockey for position on the issue of the strike. On September 7, on the floor of the Rhode Island State Senate, Democratic Minority Leader William Troy, told his colleagues his party "should brook no intimidation by local or State Police, and absolutely no military oppression in any form." The Majority Leader, Republican Harry T. Bodwell, responded by claiming Troy was trying to politicize the strike. Bodwell told the Senate "In the crisis that has arisen in the textile industry in Rhode Island as a result of the strike of workers, I feel the attitude of the Democratic party should be made manifest beyond cavil." Troy angrily responded to Bodwell, saying that he stood "uncompromisingly with the men and women who are fighting a battle for a living wage, decent treatment as to hours of labor and working conditions, and the recognition of their organized unions in the matter of bargaining with the mill owners." He went on to say:

"The idea of flaunting steel helmets and guns in the face of men and women instead of calming them may incite excitement which might lead to dangerous results. These people have a right to proceed in peaceful surroundings and the mill barons should not be allowed to use either the State Police or the National Guard to intimidate them.[86]

By Friday, September 7, clashes between workers and authorities at Rhode Island mills were reported. Large groups of pickets formed from flying squadrons, groups of workers travelling from factory in caravans of cars and trucks, forced the Belmont and Manchester Mills of Woonsocket, Rhode Island, to shut down apparently against the wishes of both the workers and the mill owners. In Westerly, the owners of the George C. Moore Company successfully applied for a restraining order against pickets and at the Hope Mill in Scituate, Rhode Island, pickets surrounded local police Chief John Riley, who, fearing for his safety, drew his gun to escape from the picketers and immediately called the State Police for backup. When State Police Captain Jonathan Harwood arrived at the Hope Mill, UTW organizer Joseph Sylvia was there with pickets massing around the entry of the plant, not allowing anything or anyone in or out of the plant. As a result, Harwood issued an order, apparently meant to be carried out statewide, limiting only four union pickets per location. Catching Sylvia off guard with the sweeping order, he immediately went to Providence to meet with Attorney General Hartigan, who informed Sylvia that no such command had been authorized.[87]

Seemingly not satisfied with Hartigan's word, Sylvia rushed to the State House and demanded an audience with Governor Green and tried to convince the governor that the UTW was keeping their ranks in order and peaceful picketing should not be restrained. If there was any trouble it was being brought in from out of state, likely Connecticut, and not authorized by the union. Sylvia told Green that he could not be held responsible for the actions of the flying squadrons as long as the four-picket limit remained in place.[88] After about an hour-long conference, Governor Green's office issued the following statement:

"Ex-Senator John H. Powers, vice president of the United Textile Workers of America and connected with the National Labor Board, and Mr. Joseph Sylvia of the United Textile Workers of America, requested a conference this afternoon with the governor. Attorney General Hartigan was also present. They conferred for over an hour on means for maintaining order during the strike and in especial legal, peaceful picketing in their rights at the same time the workers theirs. Messrs. Powers and Silvia had assured him that was against the policy of the strikers to allow anyone to come from outside the state in connection with picketing or to countenance the commission of any breaches of the peace. The governor stated that all present had felt hopeful that good would result from the conference."[89]

The statement was not only premature, but it would also become clear the UTW officials did not have the ability to back-up such assurances to Governor Green.

As the evening shift workers started to arrive at the Saylesville bleachery on Friday, September 7, they were greeted by hundreds of picketers. The Saylesville plant was ready for picketers to arrive because a day earlier the Saylesville plant posted a notice on the company bulletin board warning workers of pending pickets. The announcement alerted workers the company was warned about the arrival of pickets and deputy sheriffs had been hired to protect the plant. Workers could use the company cafeteria to eat "at rates calculated to suit the emergency."[90]

While waiting for the Friday night shift to start, picketers assembled at the corner of Walker and Chapel Streets, across the street from the main gate of the plant and began taunting the workers showing up for work. Inside the gate, Deputy Sheriff Herman Paster assembled a force of about twenty men and stared down the picketers. It is important to note that the opposing sides were only a narrow streets' width apart from each other, with the picketers controlling high ground of an embankment on the edge of Walker Street in front of what used to be the company clubhouse. Paster and his fellow deputies were not official law enforcement officers but were hired directly by the Saylesville plant to provide strike security. This informal army was not there to keep the peace, but to serve the interests of their employer.

From the picketers' side of the road, a group of boys began hurling rocks at the deputies. One of the UTW's picket captains, Theodore Brunelle, was injured in the melee, hit in the stomach by flying rocks. UTW vice president John Powers ordered the boys to stop and they did.[91] In the lull, Paster stepped forward and while brandishing his revolver, said "You'll get this if you don't stop that." Out of the silence a voice from the crowd rose, shouting in response "We can take it." Suddenly another barrage of rocks flew towards the deputies, striking several. About a half dozen deputies then charged the crowd, riot sticks wailing away indiscriminately. Newspaper reports gleefully describe the deputies ``laying about them with their sticks thwacking the heads and shoulders of the leaders." Four of the crowd went down with injuries; Harvey Jabotte of Central Falls, James Muirhead of Saylesville, Archie Tremblay of Lincoln and Adelard Archambault of Providence.[92] Considering the addresses of the victims, doubt can be raised about the UTW's claim that any picket line trouble was caused by outsiders from Connecticut. It is not clear what relationship, if any, the rock throwing boys had to the picketers but as we shall see, the picketers had no relationship to the Saylesville facility.

The pickets retreated, regrouped, and surged again towards the deputies. Paster ordered his men inside the plant gates to blast the pickets with a 200-pound pressure hose, driving them away from the gate. In what would foreshadow the advance and parry of the opposing sides over the next week, once out of range of the hoses, the strikers reassembled and pushed forward once again; so, Paster once again ordered them pushed back with the water. As the chaos worsened, local strike leader and UTW organizer Adelard Gingras stepped forward out of the crowd and demanded Paster take him to speak with the plant Superintendent Harold Reno. A truce of sorts settled in as Gingras entered the plant just long enough to demand Reno shut the mill down, a demand bluntly rebuffed by Reno. He told Gingras the plant would continue to operate "as long as the workers wished to continue working." Maybe Gingras knew what his answer was going to be and was simply buying time to let both sides cool off, but in any event, he returned to the picket line without any news to report other than the refusal to shut down.[93]

Shortly after Gingras' parlay with Reno, State Police Lt. Ernest Stenhouse arrived at the bleachery. He went into the facility and conferred with plant officials. Press was not invited into the meeting so there is no record of what was discussed, but Stenhouse left the brief meeting to make his way to the mill gate where he was joined by a cadre of thirteen state troopers, armed with riot sticks, revolvers, steel helmets, a machine gun and tear gas bombs. With this show of force, the troopers were able to key the picketers from pushing forward or throwing rocks.[94]

The action was not over for the day, however. As the next shift ended around 11:00, about 100 pickets were still milling about near the bleachery, using the slack time between confrontations to make their way back towards the plant gates. Once again, the picketers were attacked by the deputy sheriffs, but this time with the State Police in the vanguard, swinging their riot sticks. As the pickets retreated, strike leader Gingras was heard yelling at the police that they would be back Monday with 200 more pickets.[95]

By the end of the first week, reports were conflicting about how successful the strike was at shutting down the textile industry in Rhode Island. Newspapers reported mill owners claimed 81 mills closed with 35,000 workers idled. The UTW claimed ninety-three plants were closed with 43,000 on strike. Regardless of who was right, the strike was clearly impacting the operation of the mills, but without total shutdown, the scene was set for future confrontation. [96]

The weekend was calm in Saylesville and across Rhode Island, with only minor confrontations reported. In Richmond, picketers successfully closed the Wood River Woolen Company mill after plant superintendent William Hopwood invited picketers into the plant, telling *The Providence Journal* that "if the workers lent a willing ear to the pickets, the mill should be closed, but that if a majority of the employees insisted they wished to work, then the pickets were to withdraw." Apparently trying to outfox the superintendent and force a shutdown, the pickets refused the offer and Hopwood closed the plant "for the safety of employees."[97]

On Saturday, September 8, the UTW got a boost of support when the nearby independent union, the ITU, voted to join the strike. Joseph Schmetz, president of the ITU, said on the first day of the strike that his members would be 'standing by' but now would be joining in what he called a "good will strike."[98] The immediate effect of the ITU joining the action was to close an additional eighteen mills. Schmetz made it clear his members had "no grievances against the mill owners and would be making no demands," but would stand in solidarity with the striking UTW members. As he had stated just before the strike began, if the strike had shown some momentum, he would order his members to join the picket lines in order to increase pressure on the government to improve working conditions across the country. Apparently, Schmetz saw the momentum he was waiting for. [99]

The violence on Friday night in Saylesville forced state officials into a defensive posture. Providence Police Superintendent John Kelly issued a press release setting down a marker for the UTW. Published on the front page of the Sunday edition of *The Providence Journal*, Kelley's statement said:

> *On Tuesday Sept. 4. Joseph A Sylvia, representing himself to be the director in New England of the strike now being conducted by the United Textile Workers of America, and a Mr. Clark, a local leader of the union, made an agreement with me, in my office at police headquarters that picketing by members of the United Textile Workers of America, which they represented, would be conducted in a peaceful, orderly and lawful manner and there would be no intimidation whatsoever of workers entering or leaving the mills, and further agreed to keep their picket lines properly supervised and under the control of leaders.*
>
> *However, on many occasions since that agreement was made there has been intimidation of workers entering or leaving mills in Providence by members of picket lines. It has been obvious to the police on duty at these plants that these pickets were not under control and that illegal picketing was being carried on. [100]*

Kelly's statement is one clue about how disorganized the UTW strike was in Rhode Island.

The UTW's Sylvia was busy over the weekend rallying his troops. More than 1,500 strikers and supporters gathered for a mass rally at Miller's Pavilion in the Pawtuxet Valley near several shuttered mills. Sylvia harangued the attendees, oddly telling them that "You are as much at fault for the present working conditions as the bosses."[101] The speech seemed typical of Sylvia, who as the titular head of the strike in New England, seemed to have little control over the actions on the picket lines throughout Rhode Island and eerily foreshadowed the distance the union would eventual try to established between itself and what took place in Saylesville and elsewhere.

Governor Green spent the weekend hunkered down with advisors at the State House. Green, a Democrat, was serving his first term as governor, having won the office in 1932 after losing campaigns for the office in 1912, 1918, and 1930. Born in 1867 to one of Rhode Island's elite families (his great-great grandfather has been a member of the Continental Congress), Green's professional background was as a corporate lawyer. He began his political career as a 'reform' candidate just after the turn of the century, trying to wrest political control of the levers power from the Republican Party which had dominated Rhode Island politics since the Civil War. But with the onset of the Great Depression, Green attached himself to the Roosevelt campaign for President in 1932 and was swept into office in the Democratic sweep of that year.[102]

Organized labor was only one faction of a broad coalition of interest groups that supported Green's campaign for governor in 1932. Despite decades of political activity, Green only briefly served in elected office in 1907 and therefore did not have the opportunity to establish a legislative record on union issues. In the pre-New Deal campaign, Green's slogan was "Humanity First," based upon his belief that a key reason for the unemployment crisis of the Depression was the growing shift from human labor to machines in factory production.[103]

At the State House, Green met with the Attorney General, the Superintendent of the State Police, and the Adjutant General of the National Guard to discuss what preparations were underway for the strike and potential violence. He prepared a statement that would appear in the media on Monday, September 10, saying that picketing would only be "allowed if it were peaceful and without distress, if pickets were officially designated by their leaders and properly identified by some marking." Sensing his administration faced criticism for how it responded to the events in Saylesville and elsewhere, Governor Green defended himself, citing the lack of violence on the day after the flare up in Saylesville, and claiming it was "hard, therefore, to understand the few criticisms that have been directed at the State Police and myself." He seemed to insinuate the fear of violence was being ginned up by forces ready to deploy "extreme and arbitrary measures in mere anticipation of violence." He urged calm and tried to position his administration neutrally between the picketers and the mill owners.[104]

While Green seemed to think the worst was behind him, the owners of the Saylesville bleachery prepared for additional trouble. More deputy sheriffs were added to Herman Paster's outfit during the evening of Sunday, September 9. Paster told the press there would be no picketing allowed near the bleachery, believing his reading of the riot act on Friday gave him sweeping powers of enforcement. "That's the law," Paster told *The Providence Journal*, "and the law will be enforced."[105]

THE STRIKE ESCALATES

On the morning of September 10, with a small army of armed men patrolling the exterior of the plant, the company posted a notice to its employees reading "The objective which the leaders of the strikers have set for themselves is to shut this Plant down. They have no hostility or grievance against the Plant or its employees but in order to accomplish a complete shutdown of <u>ALL</u> Plants, have tried to force us to stop all work." Describing the situation as a "war," bleachery management rearranged work schedules and secured transportation for their workers to and from the plant.[106]

For most of the day it was quiet near the bleachery, but on Monday afternoon tensions flared once again. Two workers leaving the day shift were spotted by picketers as they walked out of the mill towards Central Falls. At the corner of Lonsdale Avenue and Walker Street, near where the action took place on Friday night, a group of picketers surrounded the workers, while other pickets, now numbering in the hundreds, cheered them on.[107] One of the picketers got in the face of the leaving workers and started to boo at them. One of the departing workers punched the picket and a fight started.[108] As the State Police rushed into the crowd in a phalanx to rescue the trapped workers, the pickets let loose with a hail of rocks. Lt. Stenhouse ordered his men to charge the pickets, pushing back many of them with tear gas grenades. About forty pickets were still engaged with the workers, forcing the State Police to wheel around and push through them in a wedge formation.[109]

It is this incident that scholar James Findlay describes as the point of no return for the violence in Saylesville.[110] Findlay describes "[t]he manhandling of strikers by deputy sheriffs was a major factor leading to the outbreak of violence, especially at Saylesville, where the conflict occurred only a week after the strike began."[111] But I disagree with his assessment that "From the onset the strike seemed well organized in Rhode Island, partly because the UTW itself was relatively well organized in the State."[112] I read the primary source material to reveal the UTW to be less well organized than he claims, in part, evidenced by their inability to truly shut down the industry in the state . Though the numbers were in dispute between the UTW and *The Providence Journal*, by the end of the first week of the strike, at best only about half of the state's cotton mills were closed.[113]

Findlay also argues the violence at Saylesville escalated because of a struggle for power between the strikers and management. He writes, "The steady escalation of conflict and violence in Saylesville from September 10 to September 12 was caused by several factors. Among the most important was the strikers' determination to force the closing of the Sayles complex."[114] But why was this mill so important? For example, less than a mile away, thousands of workers for the J. & P. Coats and Company were still working and sent a petition to Governor Green, signed by 97.5 percent of the workforce, asking for state protection so they could go to work "unmolested.[115]" Other bleacheries, including the Lincoln Bleachery in the nearby village of Lonsdale, also did not join the strike. Findlay does not explain why the Saylesville plant was so important.

As the tear gas saturated the area, pickets retreated down Lonsdale Avenue covering their eyes. Two local boys, Richard and Robert Blais, 1-year old twins, were evacuated from their house in the neighborhood, overcome by the fumes. Another local woman, Anna Hayden, collapsed from the gas exposure and was transported to the hospital.[116] While the attack was underway, a United Electric Railway trolley was forced to stop in the middle of the maelstrom and its passengers were forced to abandon their ride and flee.[117]

On the streets of Saylesville, the situation was again escalating out of control. With the State Police leading the way, pushing back the bulk of the picketers, the deputy sheriffs, joined by twenty members of the Central Falls police force, guarded the main gate of the plant. Under a new onslaught of rocks launched by picketers who had managed to double-back away from the State Police through the Moshassuck Cemetery, the deputy sheriffs opened fire on them with their riot guns -- essentially sawed-off shotguns. Four workers went down - Lionel Costa of Pawtucket, Armand Gervais of Central Falls, and Daniel McKeon of Pawtucket were shot while Louis Fercki of Pawtucket suffered a fractured skull. McKeon suffered a buckshot wound in his shoulder while Costa and Gervais had small arms wounds in their lower backs.[118]

While the wounded were transported two miles away to Notre Dame Hospital in Central Falls, police swept in to make arrests. Three men were captured: Fred Najjar, 30, identified at the time as a Syrian immigrant living in Pawtucket, Michael Barlik, 24, of nearby South Attleboro, Massachusetts, and Mathews De Sa Carvalho, 20, also of Pawtucket. The men were brought to the Lincoln State Police Barracks. *The Providence Journal* reported Najjar had a rock in his pants pockets when he was searched in the barracks and that he was "unable to account for it."[119]

A thunderstorm rolled through the area around 6 p.m., driving the crowd away.[120] As the streets cleared, a public works crew deployed to sweep the streets of leftover rocks from the encounter in front of the gate while the State Police established a front line at the corner of Walker Street and Lonsdale Ave. They strung barbed wire across the street and mounted a machine gun in the direction of the strikers who were pushed through what was now a no-man's land between the State Police and the Moshassuck Cemetery. Travel was banned in the area, creating the sense of a war zone in the neighborhood.[121]

As order was restored, High Sheriff Jonathan Andrews rushed to the State House to meet with Governor Green. On his way into the meeting, Andrews told *The Providence Journal*: "I think the situation will get worse out there. My men have been on duty 24 hours a day since last Thursday and they are about at the end of their endurance. I can't speak for the State Police, but I know they had a hard day and I doubt they would be able to go through another one as hard."[122] He delivered a personal report to the governor, reviewing what took place on Friday night and what had only recently happened again in Saylesville, and recommended he dispatch the National Guard to the scene. His note to Governor Green read in part: "I am firmly convinced that the services of the militia are required and I therefore request you order out immediately sufficient troops to suppress such mob and to prevent the perpetration of further acts of violence and a possible loss of life."[123]

Governor Green spent the evening conferencing with many of the state's elected leaders and in the evening addressed the state in a radio broadcast. Again, trying to carve a middle path, the governor told the people of Rhode Island the violence was a result of a clash of two opposing forces: one was the communists, who in Green's words "at least had the virtue of sincerity." The other force was the "reactionaries," who were looking for an excuse to unleash reprisals. Interestingly, in a dispute with the pro-management *The Providence Journal*, the newspaper refused to print all of Green's remarks because he would not release a full transcript.[124] There was no evidence to support Green's claim that "the communists" had anything to do with the violence in Saylesville but as we shall see, multiple players would start to lay the blame on them. It is also unclear who Green considered "the reactionaries." William McLoughlin's *Rhode Island: A History*, briefly mentions the strike and offers a tantalizing tidbit about how the American Legion and the Ku Klux Klan "announced that they would take care of any outside agitators who entered the state," but it seems more likely that Green, himself a former lawyer for the mill barons, was referring to the owners of the mills.[125] And as we will see later, at least one person on the management team at the Saylesville bleachery was an archetypical reactionary.

While Governor Green continued to hunker down in the State House, at 10:30 that night, 500 picketers tried to storm the mill. Under the cover of darkness, picketers had a natural advantage against the well-armed police force in front of them. The State Police had arranged for boxes of ammunition to be delivered to the picket lines and part of the arsenal included Very lights, a type of sighting flare soldiers used on the front lines in the trench warfare of World War 1 to spot enemy soldiers crossing no man's land. The police fired the Very lights into the sky and fired tear gas into the crowd as the picketers attacked the police with stones, though no further victims were reported.[126] Adding to the mayhem, pickets started pulling fire alarms in boxes lining the streets of Saylesville and Central Falls. Under the lights and gas, residents started to flee the neighborhood.[127]

At 4:00 on the morning of Tuesday, September 11, General Dean's troops began to assemble at two armories in Providence - the North Main Street Armory and the Cranston Street Armory. Meanwhile, Governor Green drafted legislation giving him the authority to increase the number of State Police officers during "actual or threatened rioting or serious breaches of the peace." Green sent the draft bill to the General Assembly, along with a request for $25,000 to fund the initiative. In another radio broadcast later that evening, Green told the people of Rhode Island, "To make it clear, it is not the intention that these men shall be added to the force for the purpose of breaking the present strike, but only for the protection of all parties, directly or indirectly interested - strikers, workers, employees, and the general public."[128]

While Green maneuvered, the Saylesville bleachery braced for more attacks. The company posted another notice to workers, laying out their interpretation of events. To the plant managers, the trouble was clearly caused by the union leaders who were bent on forcing the plant to close. They told their workers effective the following day, the hours of work would change from a three, 8-hour shift format to a two, 12-hour shift system.[129] Later in the day new reporters began to assemble near the plant in set up a base camp in a shop called Brodeur's, at 1101 Lonsdale Avenue, directly in between the State Police barrier at the corner of Walker and Lonsdale and the gates of the Moshassuck Cemetery where the picketers encamped. Sheriff Andrews used the same building as a command center; so, the reporters essentially were now embedded with the Sheriff's troops.[130]

The State Police continue to patrol the perimeter they established at the corner of Walker and Lonsdale Avenue and reinforced their position by stationing Corporal Robert Burns, a World War I veteran, with a machine gun on top of the bleachery roof. The Central Falls Police Department assembled under the command of Chief George Collette and stationed themselves with the State Police at the Walker Street intersection. Andrew's deputies stationed themselves by the corner of Lonsdale and Conduit Street, in front of a company gate leading into a filtration plant. [131]

Slowly, as the afternoon progressed, the crowd in the streets of Saylesville began to build in size. With the various combatants from the night before back in their respective corners, one can imagine each faction looking over the vacant space between them wondering who or what would set things in motion again today. The spark was lit around 3:00 when a dump truck from the Durastone Company, located on the back side of the plant's property, turned left from Higginson Avenue onto Lonsdale Avenue with a truck load of bricks destined for a Pawtucket City Hall construction project. As the truck lumbered past the picketers and into the no man's land it was abruptly stopped by the people on the street. While the driver, Peter Beretta, was taken out of the truck cab and roughed up by a handful of picketers, others swarmed onto the truck and began to hand its cargo down to their comrades on the street.[132]

While the police rushed to get the truck out of the way and back on the road, the newly armed pickets turned on the deputy sheriffs guarding the gate to the bleachery's filtration plant. Under a fusillade of brick, the deputies momentarily retreated, giving the picketers just enough time to crash through the gate guarding the filtration plant and tear down a guard shack. Chaos erupted. The Central Falls police rushed to the corner of Conduit Street, leaving the State Police behind because their orders did not allow them to leave the Lincoln side of Saylesville. While they sprinted to the scene, at 3:12 the first shots of the day were fired by the deputy sheriffs. Three pickets went down. Mrs. Leonie Gussart, 73, of Pawtucket, was shot with a riot gun in the shins, Ernest LeGrade, 28, and Wilfred Plante, 32, both of Pawtucket, were shot in the legs. An unnamed picket was clubbed in the head while another unnamed woman was carried away in a hysterical fit, screaming repeatedly "I'm afraid, I'm afraid." The wounded were again transported to Notre Dame Hospital.[133]

During the chaos, Rocky Martell, President of the Central Falls City Council and a resident of Lonsdale Avenue near where the battle was taking place tried his best to direct traffic which was, incredibly, still travelling up and down the street. Because the State Police had Walker Street barricaded, the trackless trolley had to travel farther down Lonsdale Avenue than usual on temporary wires. At one point in the commotion a car jumped the sidewalk and nearly crushed a group of young people who were standing on the sidewalk watching the action. Within minutes the police and sheriffs started to drive the crowd back towards the cemetery gates.[134]

As the attack unfolded, Sheriff Andrews, from his post inside Brodeur's store, called Governor Green and asked for help from the militia. The reporters in the room overheard a heated conversation with the governor and reported Andrews saying, "You want to wait until something happens. I want to protect the people who want to go to work," clearly indicated which side of the conflict his allegiances lay. When Andrews hung up, he turned to the press corps and said "Well, it's on his shoulders if they all get killed out there." After the assault at Conduit Street, Andrews was back on the phone to Governor Green: "It's on your head, governor, if you don't send those troops to Saylesville. They've broken down the gate and I don't know what they are going to do next." On this word, Governor Green called General Dean and gave him the order to deploy.[135]

There were close to 3,000 people on the streets of Saylesville at this point. An aid to Governor Green rushed to Sheriff Andrews location to tell him the Guard was on the way and to contact the governor immediately. When Andrews phoned the governor, he was informed that he was being relieved from duty.[136] Perhaps because he saw the huge crowd on the street gear up for action or perhaps because in his opinion he did not report to the governor but instead reported to his paymasters at the Saylesville bleachery, Andrews told the governor's aid that he would "take that under advisement." He then called Robert B. Dresser, the attorney for the factory, and told him that the militia was on the way. Dresser instructed the company to tell the sheriffs to return to the barracks inside the factory gates until a decision was made, by the company, if they wanted the sheriffs to remain on duty.[137]

While Andrews' deputy sheriffs retreated, the militia mustered to bugle calls and boarded trucks to head to Saylesville. One hundred men of the 103rd Field Artillery, commanded by Col. Harold Baker, were given a police escort out of Providence for the five-mile drive to Saylesville. A second detail of 150 soldiers from the 243rd Coast Artillery under the command of Col. John Collins left the nearby Cranston Street Armory. Among the soldiers were several recent graduates of Brown University, and the University's alumni magazine later boasted of the 'legendary' service of their graduates, who provided both aerial and other surveillance for the militia.[138]

The troops arrived in Saylesville at 4:10 and unloaded from their trucks in relative silence. However, as the last truck pulled into the area the crowd started to boo the soldiers and as they finished deploying the rocks started to fly. For five minutes, the Guard withstood the barrage of stones while they formed up in orderly lines of ten men each. Suddenly, an officer's whistle blew, and the Guardsmen attacked the crowd, indiscriminately swinging riot clubs at whomever was in their way.[139]

People fled down side streets and through the backyards of the neighborhood. *The Providence Journal* described the attack on the pickets gleefully: "In a few cases their pursuers were fleeter.

Down came the clubs. Girls and women scurried for cover, shrieking as though they were departing for all time, but soon quiet prevailed."[140] After the crowd retreated to safety, they regrouped and pushed back against the Guard. For the rest of the afternoon this pattern of assault and counter assault continued. In one push by the soldiers, they shot a volley of rifle fire over the heads of the pickets, which forced them back to the Dexter Street intersection. Incredibly, during the fray, the soldiers dropped a box of tear gas bombs that was picked up by the pickets. The people promptly began to throw the bombs back at the Guard itself, pushing them back to the Walker Street barricade. Flummoxed, the Guard switched to nausea gas and made another push. The entire neighborhood was poisoned with the gas, sending the Blais twins to the hospital for a second day in a row.[141]

At around 6:00 that evening, the Guard, outmatched on the street, called for reinforcements. All Guardsmen across the state were ordered to muster at their home armories and await orders. General Dean would not comment about how many soldiers he had at his disposal, but the reports were the entire Guard comprised 550 soldiers and 50 officers. Since he was himself in the field, General Dean had to improvise in how his order was to be conveyed to his men. In Newport, Company F of the 118th Engineers, was called to duty with two rounds of nine blows of the fire alarm horn. Other troops mustered after hearing a radio broadcast calling them to duty, which *The Providence Journal* reported was 80% effective. [142]

At 7:00, the reinforcements arrived. The 153rd Hospital Company set up a field station behind the factory gates under the command of Major Earle Brennan to treat the wounded militiamen. As the militia moved to surround the entire bleachery area the pickets regrouped on their side of no man's land. As daylight waned, the parish priest from St. Mathieu's Church at the corner of Dexter and Lonsdale Streets pleaded with Central Falls Police Chief George Collette to get the picketers off the church grounds. Collette was refused help from the Guard in this task, so with his twenty-two men he tried to get the pickets to withdraw from the church property. He was aided by Theodore Brunelle from the UTW. Brunelle jumped atop a car and pleaded with the crowd to withdraw.[143]

Whether the crowd was following the orders of Collette and Brunelle, or whether they simply took a dinner break, the pickets did not launch another major attack until just before 10:00 that night when they attacked the soldiers at three points. One attack happened directly in front of the Moshassuck Cemetery, where some soldiers were stationed. Another at the corner of Lonsdale and Liberty Streets, where the Sheriffs patrolled, guarding the area where the pickets earlier torn down the gate. The third was at the State Police barricade at Walker and Lonsdale. Learning from their better armed adversaries, the pickets fired Roman candles into the air to acting improvised Very lights. At least one soldier, Captain John C. Ball, was injured significantly enough in the battle in the cemetery with a head wound that he had to be transported to the field hospital for treatment.[144]

While all this was going on, Joseph Sylvia from the UTW finally appeared on the picket line in Saylesville. He drove his car to the rear side of the militia lines and asked to speak with General Dean. After keeping him waiting for 30 minutes, the General agreed to speak with Sylvia inside the factory gates in the Guard's makeshift barracks. While Dean and Sylvia were cloistered in the barracks for over an hour, the battle intensified on the street. The soldiers and police, caught off guard by the ferocity of the attack, again flooded the area with gas. The Guard could no longer stop the crowd from advancing with the gas bombs, so an order was dispatched back to the armory for an order of more ammunition. Sylvia and Dean finished their conference without comment to the press. Sylvia left the picket line area and Dean resumed his position at the command post.[145]

The battle continued for several more hours. At 12:30 in the morning, the pickets were finally able to knock out the last remaining streetlight at the corner of Tucker Street, casting the whole battle zone into complete darkness. With extra cover, the pickets intensified their attack. This time, General Dean himself led the Guardsmen's counter offensive, driving the pickets back again into the grounds of the cemetery. At 1:15, the 243rd Coast Artillery unit deployed three anti-aircraft lights, adding to the warfare like atmosphere in the streets. At 2:00, a cohort of 300 pickets, including several "young girls and youths" marched down Lonsdale Avenue toward the line of the Guardsmen. The pickets taunted the soldiers, daring them to shoot. One woman, it was reported, stood in front of the crowd, trying to provoke the armed militia men, daring them to shoot her where she stood. In a notable shift, newspaper reports described the hostile crowd as hurling "communist rhetoric" at the soldiers, cursing the government while the soldiers "stood silent under epithets and jeers."[146] After almost 12 hours of continuous fighting, the pickets started to slip away, but not before removing all the manhole covers on Liberty Street and opening up the fire hydrants, flooding the underground wire channels. By 3:00 in the morning the streets were empty, and what *The Pawtucket Times* was already referring to as "The Battle of Moshassuck Cemetery" was over.[147]

During the day, at least fifty pickets were injured, including three who were shot. Among the injured was Peter Szeliga, a 19-year-old Central Falls man who was treated at Notre Dame Hospital for first degree burns on his hand after he picked up an unexploded gas bomb and it blew up in his hand. Seven Guardsmen were injured, including Private Chester Bromley of the 103rd Field Artillery, who suffered powder burns on his hand when he picked up one of the Guard's lost gas bombs the pickets had commandeered for their defense. Seven people were arrested, all of whom lived in the general vicinity of the strike area but none of whom worked at the Saylesville plant. Newspaper reports claim that during the entire day, nearly the entire workforce of the bleachery reported to work.[148]

With the situation on the streets out of control, Governor Green made another radio broadcast to the people of Rhode Island. As Green's biographer Erwin L. Levine emphasizes in *Theodore Francis Green, the Rhode Island Years*, the governor desperately wanted to keep order while not being accused of breaking the strike.[149] Green's predecessor, Emery San Souci, lost his bid for re-election after ordering the National Guard to attack strikers during the 1922 textile strike. Governor Green told his constituents, "order must be restored - not in the interest of the plant, not in the interest of any particular group, but in the interest of the safety of the state of Rhode Island." The day before Green blamed the violence on both communists and reactionaries, this time he placed the blame on the sheriffs. He told the people:

"What a difference between the record of the State Police in this emergency and the record of the deputy sheriffs; the contrast between doing things the right way and doing things the wrong way. The State Police have not fired a shot. Everyone one of the persons - men and women- were shot down by the deputy sheriffs - not due to the individual man as much as to the system- men untrained and unsuited for this delicate work, armed with guns, who in many cases pushes into the crowd with rough words cause [sic] intentional provocation.[150]"

The governor also expressed exasperation with Sheriff Andrews. After ordering him and his men to stand down, Andrews told him he had to consult with mill ownership before complying with the order. "He meant, I suppose," Governor Green said, "Mr. Robert B. Dresser. In other words, the order of the governor in this emergency is subject to the veto of Mr. Robert B. Dresser."[151]

Dresser, the lawyer for the bleachery, was the archetypal reactionary in Green's now abandoned "both sides" argument. Throughout the strike he served as spokesperson for the Sayles Finishing Plant and, as Green's comments indicate, directed the actions of Sheriff Andrews and his deputies. Dresser was a long-time conservative activist, later becoming a member of the John Birch Society, and regularly publishing right-wing broadsides in conservative and libertarian magazines like *The Freeman* and *The Committee for Constitutional Government*.[152] In the late 1950's and early 1960's he led the opposition in Rhode Island against laws aimed at prohibiting housing discrimination against African-Americans.[153] When he died at age 95 in 1976, the *New York Times* wrote of him, "He believed the Federal Government was destroying the private enterprise system through taxation."[154]

As James Findlay confirms in his essay, eyewitness reports in the press clearly indicate the deputy sheriffs were provoking the violence from the pickets. Former State Representative Arthur Costigan who lived in the neighborhood told reporters he would be filing a formal protest over the 'provocative methods' used by the sheriffs, including pointing their guns at pickets without reason. At another point in the melee a deputy sheriff threw a tear gas bomb through the window of Brodeur's store, injuring *Providence Journal* photographer George Goodreau and sending the rest of the press corps scrambling for cover.[155] But simply transferring command of the streets from the sheriffs to the militia did little to quell the uprising.

The deputy sheriffs were gone from the streets of Saylesville on the morning of September 12. In their place were fresh National Guard troops who moved immediately to assert their presence. At 6:00 in the morning, with hundreds of pickets assembled on the Central Falls side of Lonsdale Avenue, next to St. Mathieu's Church, the Guard issued an order to disperse. When the pickets refused to move, the Guard fired their rifles over the heads of the crowd. General Dean was later asked if he had given orders to his men to "shoot to kill?" "No," he said, but ominously added "the bullets just missed."[156] After the shooting, Col. Herbert Barker of the 103rd led thirty-two of his men onto the grounds of Moshassuck Cemetery, with bayonets mounted on their rifles, to track down a group of suspected ring leaders of the pickets who had fled for protection from the gunshots behind gravestones. A volley of rifle fire, some ripping through headstones, forced the hiding pickets out from cover and back onto the street, where they were apprehended by the guardsmen. Ten people, including 16-year-old Rita Brouilette of Central Falls, were marched single file by the soldier to an awaiting truck that transported them to the Lincoln police station.[157]

Shortly before 7:00, seven more truckloads of troops arrived on the scene. The soldiers were detailed to clean up the considerable debris off Lonsdale Ave from the battle the day before. As the soldiers began to station themselves at their posts, pickets jeered at them, telling them to "go home and do the housekeeping" and "you'd shoot your own mother." The crowd continued to swell, as did the number of troops, now reported to be a force of 1,200 strong. At 10:00, General Dean ordered sharpshooters stationed at the gates of Moshassuck Cemetery sending a clear message they were preparing for a serious confrontation and not to be trifled with.[158]

With the troops massing on the street, the Saylesville community began to show signs of battle fatigue. St. Mathieu's parochial school and the West Side grammar school across the street from St. Mathieu's Church released their pupils early with instructions to go home. Rev. Peter Hanley of nearby Holy Trinity Church told his parochial school pupils they too would be released early. But if the schools had hoped releasing the students would get them to safety from what they feared the Guard was gearing up for, they were mistaken. The students, at least some of the older ones, appear to have joined the crowd of pickets, swelling their numbers even further.[159]

While the schools were shutting down, General Dean and his men dug in. Around 11:00 in the morning, the 118th Engineering Company dug holes in the street and erected wooden posts to connect barbed wire in what Harold Fletcher, a National Guardsman at the time of the troubles, described as a French high-wire double apron, affectionately known as a 'gooseberry.[160] But while the troops were digging in, carloads of new picketers began to arrive. However, unlike the mass of people at the other end of Lonsdale Avenue, these pickets seemed organized. The 140 people were all wearing white armbands and collected themselves in teams of twenty. They approached the Guard barricade and asked to be let through so they could picket in front of the factory gate. However, Col. Harold Baker refused them safe passage.[161]

A man stood out from the crowd and told Col. Baker his

name was William Clark of Providence and that he was an organizer for the UTW. According to Clark, he and his official pickets had been authorized under an agreement with the governor and the union to allow groups of 20 pickets, duly recognizable by their white armbands, to picket during daylight hours. Baker still refused passage. Within minutes, Joseph Sylvia arrived on the scene and confirmed Clarke's story about a deal being made with Governor Green. Baker still refused passage to the group.[162] This group of authorized union pickets was the first sign of organized activity by the UTW since Friday evening.

While the UTW tangled with Baker and the Guard, Governor Green sought to gain control of the political situation. That morning he delivered a letter to Sheriff Andrews asking for the names of all the men who had served as deputy sheriffs at the Saylesville plant. Apparently reacting to the reports of the misadventures of the armed deputies, Governor Green told Andrews to "Consider this an order, not a request."[163] The governor met again with General Dean, who apprised him of the situation. While they were meeting, reports came to the State House that the crowd was growing again in Saylesville. Dean rushed back to the scene and the governor issued the following statement:

"The situation in Saylesville is still serious. General Dean and I have been conferring in my office and were interrupted by news that the mob was collecting again and he immediately left to take command there. Order must be reestablished in the interest of all - the workers, the mill owners and you, the people of the state. Please try to realize this; realize also that you have a duty to perform. The large number of people not connected with the strike who congregated about the Saylesville bleachery yesterday and last night added to the disorder and made it difficult for the National Guard to do their work properly. Practically all, if not all, of the persons arrested proved to be neither former workers of the mill nor strikers; they were curiosity seekers or hoodlums. I beg of you all to keep away from that neighborhood. No one should go there unless absolutely

obliged to do so. Every curiosity seeker adds to the confusion. He not only runs the risk of injury and possible loss of life, if shots are to be fired, but also, he adds to the danger of others. Let everyone help in this emergency and one way of helping is by keeping away from places of disorder, keep away yourself, and urge everyone else to keep away. I ask for your help and am confident it will be given."[164]

As General Dean left the State House, he issued an ominous statement to the assembled press:

"My men have taken severe punishment for 14 hours. They have been the target for rocks of all kinds and sizes, but from now on there will be no more rock throwing. We are not going to tolerate any further hurling of such things. The moment rock throwing starts we will act much differently than we have up to this point".[165]

As in the previous days there was a midday lull in the action on the streets before, midway through the afternoon, the opposing sides geared up for battle. The soldiers began to spread more barbed wire across Lonsdale Ave at the corner of Liberty street, essentially cutting the 'no man's land' between the Guard's line and the picketers' line in half.[166] As the Guardsmen locked themselves into position, about 500 pickets marched up the streets towards them. As the hot summer sun beat down on the combatants, rocks started to fly at the soldiers. The pickets began to improvise with their weapons, filling bottles with nails and screws, and even stringing a rubber inner tube from a car tire in between two tree limbs at the corner of Moshassuck cemetery to use as a giant slingshot.[167] As the barrage opened up, one guardsman, William Castaldi, was hit in the head with a flowerpot flung from the slingshot.[168]

As promised by General Dean, the Guardsmen showed no tolerance for the attack. Four soldiers armed with rifles deployed to the corner of the barbed wire post and the order to fire was given. The soldiers fired indiscriminately into the crowd, which had now grown to nearly 5,000 people. The crowd panicked and ran for cover into the cemetery, breaking off pieces of headstones to fling back at the pursuing Guardsmen. Two teenage boys ducked for cover behind two of the gravestones close to the street and raised handkerchiefs as white flags, and they were dragged to safety behind the soldiers' line. After the volley of shots, the guard used "gas guns" to shoot tear and nausea gas at the pickets, blanketing the entire area again with noxious fumes. The crowd retreated as best they could back to the Central Falls side of Lonsdale Avenue, picking up their wounded along the way.[169]

Three people were shot. Nicholas Gravello, 22, of Pawtucket, was shot through the right arm, Charles Gorcynski, 18, of Central Falls, was shot in the stomach and William Blackwood, 44, of Pawtucket, was shot in the head. Unlike the previous shooting victims, who had been hit with buck shot from deputy sheriffs, these men were hit with rifle fire. The wounded were rushed to Notre Dame Hospital where it was clear that Gorcynski and Blackwood were in grave condition. Father St. Goddard of Notre Dame Church performed the Last Rights on Gorcynski while Blackwood's mother collapsed when she arrived at the hospital discovering her son was shot. Witnesses told reporters neither man was directly connected to the strike. Gorcynski was employed at another nearby mill and was the sole breadwinner for his family, including eight brothers and sisters. Blackwood, an unemployed weaver, had gone to the picket line looking for his 18-year-old son who was reportedly involved in the action.[170]

As reports started to filter back to the lines about the fate of the wounded, General Dean told reporters that his "men went out with the intention of shooting anybody who did not obey their orders."[171] With open warfare in the streets, the community leaders in the area demanded an end to hostilities. Robert Briden, president of the Board of Trustees of Moshassuck cemetery fired off a terse telegram to Governor Green demanding his cemetery be protected. The message read:

The Board of Trustees of Moshassuck Cemetery demand protection for the graves of our loved ones who are interred in this sacred ground. We appeal to you as governor to prevent the desecration that has taken place during the past few days.[172]

The Pawtucket Common (i.e., City) Council was more demanding of Green. They met in emergency session and passed the following resolution:

Whereas the Pawtucket Common Council interested in the welfare of the citizens of this city and the peace of this city and neighboring communities, urge the governor to use whatever power he may have under the Constitution and laws to close mills in areas where bloodshed is like to occur and to proceed with qualified and representative officials on both sides of this controversy to bring about peace, law, and order in the State of Rhode Island.[173]

The Central Falls Common Council sent a similar resolution with the same demand – shut down the Saylesville plant to avoid future bloodshed.[174]

With Saylesville now fully embroiled in virtual hand-to-hand combat, the UTW leaders scrambled about what to do next. Sylvia demanded another audience with Governor Green and General Dean returned from the front for the meeting. There is no record of what was said in their conference, but as the rioting intensified in Saylesville, Governor Green issued an order to be read on the streets. The responsibility fell to Central Falls Police Lt. Joseph Chaput, who read the following statement from the governor to the crowd assembled at Dexter and Lonsdale:

I do hereby charge and command all people who are unlawfully, riotously or tumultuously assembled anywhere in this State that they immediately disperse and peaceably depart to their habitations, under penalties inflicted by the laws of this state. [175]

The crowds did not disperse as ordered. With thousands of people still in the streets, Governor Green once again took to the radio waves to plea for calm. At 8:15 that evening, Green told the people of Rhode Island:

Believing that the bad feeling between the National Guard and the strikers was in reality the result of a misunderstanding, I called a conference this afternoon between high military officers and strike leaders, and I am glad beyond words to say that the conference was productive of good results and adjourned with an agreement with regard to picketing which I trust may prove to be effective. Picketing has been a great source of disagreement and violence.[176]

He also told the people of Rhode Island, that "I want to emphasize the point that this is not an armistice between opposing forces."

The pickets on the streets of Saylesville certainly did not recognize the situation for an armistice, as they continued to harass the soldiers with rocks and other projectiles. Shortly after the governor started his radio speech, the soldiers again opened fire on the crowd. One boy, Fernand LaBreche, 17, of Central Falls, was shot near the heart. As LaBreche lay bleeding on the ground, a soldier came running up to the line shouting to his comrades "Hold your fire, and agreement has been made between the governor and other officials! There will be no more firing." [177] This did little to assuage the anger of the crowd. Central Falls patrolman Alfred Viau was hit in the head with a rock and transported unconscious to Notre Dame Hospital. By 10:00 there were still thousands of people on the streets.[178]

Around 11:00, anti-aircraft lights were deployed in the

yard of the plant to give the soldiers a clearer picture of the battle-field. Seeking to establish cover, the pickets put out the lights of any car that was traveling through the area. One driver who re-fused to turn out his lights had his car seized and overturned by the pickets.[179] Whether intentional or not, when Sylvia finally returned to the scene before midnight, his car was bombarded with rocks and he was hit in the head. Sylvia, however, recovered enough to issue the following statement:

I feel confident that if the United Textile Workers of America are not victims again of broken promises that violence and dis-order will not reign again in Saylesville. Tonight, we assured Governor Green and Adjt. General Dean that we will be willing to cooperate with their military organization in keeping peace in the strike. This is the same assurance that we gave Com-manding Officer Dean last night when he agreed to allow us to have pickets in five blocks of 20 under designated captains properly identified, but this gentlemen's agreement was broken and as a result three are critically wounded and one is seriously wounded. We sent one squad of ten pickets at 10 AM today to determine the seriousness of ADJT. General Dean's agreement. We did not send the hundred, but we found drawn clubs and rifles in the hands of the guardsmen. Although properly desig-nated not a union striker was allowed inside the rope lines that preceded the barbed wire barricades. Then clubs were wielded, tear gas was hurled and shots were fired, the result of a broken agreement. If our pickets could do their part there would be no bloodshed. School children would not have been the object of stones or bullets or clubs if we had been allowed to follow out the plan which we agreed to try at the suggestion of Adjutant Dean.[180]

The people of Saylesville woke up the news that Charles Gorcynski died from his wounds. There were no picketers anywhere to be found and the National Guard troops took advantage of their absence to extend their fortifications further down Lonsdale Avenue in both directions, erecting barbed wire gateways on either end. Residents had to show identification to come or go through the gates. Seventeen men who had been arrested by the Guard over the last twenty-four hours were turned over to the Central Falls police and transported to the 11th District Court in front of Judge Charles Risk. Three of the men plead guilty to minor charges, two of whom were sentenced to thirty days in jail, and one released after paying a fine. The other fourteen pleaded innocent to the more serious charge of "riotous assembly." Their collective bond was set at $24,200. A few paid their portion of the bond, most did not, and were held over for trial scheduled for September 25.[181]

The UTW organizers gathered for a morning meeting at the Labor Temple to assess the situation. Adelard Gingras told reporters after the meeting the UTW had appointed selected men to work with the Central Falls police to identify any radical agitators who were in the area looking to cause trouble. Despite the increased Guard fortifications and the union's willingness to work with the police, a crowd of about 500 people gathered in Quinn Square, near St. Mathieu's church, around 3:00. After being ordered to leave, police arrested three men from Providence who refused to move. The show of force and the arrests dissuaded the crowd from any further action and other than a small group of people approaching the Liberty Street guard gate in the evening, all remained quiet.[182]

At 10:30 that morning, Governor Green received a call from President Roosevelt. They discussed the situation in Rhode Island and the possible deployment of federal troops to forestall any more violence. Governor Green described the call to reporters:

> President Roosevelt has just called me up, and I had a long and most satisfying talk with him. I told him the length of the situation here, and he showed remarkable knowledge of Rhode Island conditions. He said he was getting in touch with Washington to have all in-

formation ready and all preparations made to respond to any call for federal troops the state might formally make in this emergency. He ended by saying that he was heartily in back of me and would support me to the limit.[183]

Roosevelt's office also issued a statement after the call, saying: "The President is in complete and constant touch with the Rhode Island situation. It is, of course, hoped that disorders caused by irresponsible and disorderly individuals will terminate before nightfall."[184] After the call between the governor and the president it was reported General Douglas MacArthur was beginning preparations to send federal troops to the strike area and troop movements were noted across New England. Five hundred soldiers of the 13th Infantry and the 66th Tank division were ordered to cancel scheduled maneuvers and report immediately to Fort Devens, Massachusetts, an hour's drive from Saylesville. Secretary of War George Dern was also reportedly on his way to Rhode Island to arrive before President Roosevelt, who was scheduled to be in Newport that weekend for an annual yacht race.[185]

Green also spoke that morning with Saylesville Finishing Plant lawyer Robert B. Dresser. After the phone call, the Board of Directors for the Saylesville plant met and voted to close the plant effective at 5:00 that evening. Later in the day, Dresser made public a carefully worded letter to the press he had sent Green to confirm the closing. It read in part:

Although we have had no strike, and have no dispute with our own employees, who urgently need the employment which we are willing and able to afford them if given protection in continued operation, nevertheless, the board of directors conceives it as a duty in common with that of all good citizens to cooperate to the fullest extent with you as commander-in-chief of the state military force and as governor of the State in meeting the crisis which you state has arisen.

Accordingly, we beg to state that we are complying with your request and that our plant at Saylesville will be closed at 5 O'clock this afternoon, when the day shift ends.[186]

Inside the plant, the company posted two separate notices to workers, telling them that as the Commander and Chief of the State, the governor had ordered the plant closed.[187]

As the drama subsided on the streets of Saylesville, it was just beginning at the State House. Governor Green, concerned about the potential for continued violence, called an emergency session of the Rhode Island General Assembly to consider a sweeping package of bills he claimed would allow him to take control of the situation. He was aware although the use of federal troops was offered, it would take time for those troops to mobilize and transport to Rhode Island. Therefore, he submitted emergency legislation to the General Assembly doing four things: allocate an additional $100,000 to the State Police to increase their ranks, allocate an additional $100,000 to the National Guard so that they could deploy 1000 veterans immediately to strike areas, allow the Governor to close any mills in the state by executive order, and finally, declare a state of insurrection existed, empowering the governor to formally request the federal troops.[188]

The governor prepared a statement for the members of the General Assembly outlining his reasons for calling the special session. He wrote to them saying:

I have called you together here today, although you were to have met tomorrow, because of a crisis in the affairs of State. We are face to face now, not with a textile strike, but a communist uprising. What started as local conflicts between employers and striking workers over the question of picketing has grown and spread to other localities and includes a large number of persons with no interest whatsoever in the strike but seeking merely to create disorder, and some of them with the de-

liberate plan to upset our established government. [189]

He reviewed what actions his administration had taken so far to suppress this "communist uprising" including replacing the deputy sheriffs with the State Police and then supporting the State Police with the militia. He praised the actions of both, but also acknowledged that thus far these steps had "proved inadequate" to the situation. Therefore:

Due to the fact that some time will be required to select and place on active duty additional members of the State Police and in order that increased protection of our people and property by tonight, I have prepared for your consideration and passage legislation permitting this state to take advantage of the provisions of the constitution of the United States by calling for aid from the armed forces of the Federal Government.[190]

The General Assembly was divided between a House of Representatives controlled by Democrats and a Senate controlled by Republicans. Additionally, the House majority was divided into two factions: one supporting fellow Democrat Green, and another controlled by Pawtucket Democratic Party boss, and rival of Green, Thomas McCoy. McCoy and Green spent years jousting for control of the Party and at this stage of Green's first term as governor, it was not clear who had the upper hand.[191]

The special session started off in a spirit of bipartisanship, with the leaders in both chambers agreeing to waive procedural rules so the governor's proposals could be given speedy consideration. But not long after the session began, Governor Green's proposals hit a snag. The Democratic Party caucus in the House, even after the governor personally addressed them, called for tabling the measure calling for federal troops and declaring a state of insurrection. They did support his other calls for more money for the State Police and National Guard and giving him the authority to close the mills.[192]

While initially signaling he would be willing to support the governor's proposals, after a party caucus in the Senate, Republican Senate Majority Leader Bodwell told the governor he would not be able to support the measure giving the governor the authority to close any mills. Bodwell told the governor passing such a bill would make Green a 'tool of labor.'[193] When the Senate convened later in the day, Bodwell moved to divide the legislation into two separate measures - one concerning the additional funds for the State Police and National Guard, the other addressing the power to close the mills (it is unclear if the Senate ever took up the proposal to declare a state of insurrection). Democratic Minority Leader Senator William Troy, who verbally sparred with Bodwell at the outset of the strike, took to the floor of the Senate and declared that Bodwell had broken his word to the governor on the measures. Bodwell proceeded anyway with the motion to divide the question, which was authorized by the majority. He then took to the floor to explain his support for the measure for additional funds. He said:

Flames of communism and all that goes under the red banner threaten the safety of our people and the security of their homes. An extreme emergency exists. In such an emergency there is only one thing for patriotic Americans to do, and that is to join wholeheartedly, genuinely and completely in aiding the Chief Executive, in seeing that he is given the tools required - it is not a question of what kind they should be - so that the safety of our people and homes may be protected.[194]

Minority leader Troy implored his colleagues to pass both measures to no avail. When the vote was taken on the divided measure the provision to support the additional funding and manpower was approved unanimously but was 25-15, following party lines, against the mill closing bill. The Rhode Island General Assembly does not operate with a conference committee structure like the United State Congress. Instead, for a bill to become law, it must first pass in both chambers, with identical language, before it can be sent to the governor for signature or veto. However, the House had already adjourned for the day, meaning the measures would need to wait until the next day, Friday, for consideration. [195]

Although the House was adjourned, the Democratic Party again caucused privately to decide what to do next on. The next day, when the House convened shortly after 10:00 in the morning, the plan hatched in the caucus unfolded. House Majority Leader Representative Edmund Flynn took to the floor and assigned the bill to increase funding for the State Police and the National Guard to the House Finance committee, as is customary protocol. However, in a move catching Governor Green by surprise, Flynn then made a motion to adjourn. The motion was seconded by Representative Patrick McAughey, an ally of the McCoy block in the House. While members of the House aligned with the governor protested the move, the vote to adjournment was approved, effectively killing all of Green's proposals. With no legislation before them, the Senate followed the House and adjourned shortly after 1:30 that afternoon.[196]

A chastened Governor Green called the press to his office in the State House and issued the following statement:

I am very much disappointed that the House Finance Committee did not report the bill passed by the Senate which would have increased the State Police appropriation during this emergency. I was informed yesterday that certain influences in the House, which continuously have hindered legislation which I have sponsored killed this measure. Certain members of the House have informed me just what the motives of this group are. When the National Guard is withdrawn from the strike areas, which I hope will be soon, some force will have to be in readiness to augment the local police forces. The State Police are doing well to maintain their share of the work at the present time They will need assistance then. The responsibility for killing this act will lie with this group of men who I have heard before have continually blocked efforts to pass legislation that I believe to be necessary. Petty personal grievances should be overlooked at this time of great emergency. [197]

The action at the State House was not the only drama for the day. A bomb scare during the day raised concerns the situation was about to turn explosive. Police reported twenty-five sticks of dynamite were stolen from the St. James Cemetery in the Manville neighborhood of Lincoln. *The Pawtucket Times* claimed the theft was part of a communist plot to blow up the Diamond Hill Reservoir on the Cumberland/Lincoln border. Cumberland Police officer James Bradley told reporters he was contacted by residents living near the Arnold Mill complex about three cars suspiciously parked nearby so he and members of the State Police stood guard by a dam near the reservoir. Despite attributing the theft of dynamite to a "communist plot" there is no evidence to support the claim and there never was any explosion.[198]

Just before the General Assembly began its special session, Governor Green sent a telegram to every police department in the state to round up all known communists.[199] The order was the culmination of a campaign, led by the governor and supported by both the UTW, the police, and the press, to blame the disorder on the communists. Earlier in the week, police arrested nine men from Boston outside of the Roger Williams Furniture Company on Pearl Street in Providence. The men were affiliated with a union named the Independent Furniture Workers Union and detained after a search of their car revealed they had a night stick and a rubber hose, presumed by the police to be weapons. When the police took the men back to the police station for questioning, they contacted the Boston Police Department's "Radical Squad" who informed them the union the men were affiliated with was "of a distinctively radical nature" and the men were "reds." When a lawyer from Boston, Louis Gurman, arrived at the police station to secure bail for the men, he too was detained until the "Radical

Squad" in Boston confirmed his status as a lawyer.[200]

Police also told reporters they were tracking the movements of another known radical, a Brooklyn, New York, woman named Ida Alter, who was seen talking to workers in the Olneyville factory area. They referred to Alter as "an inflammatory talker and to be possessed of more education that the ordinary mill worker." Police believed she was associated with UTW organizer William Clark. The Police told reporters ``We have not connected any of these people with any communistic organization. We know, however, that some of them have decidedly radical tendencies. What develops later remains to be seen."[201]

What developed later was a raid on the Communist Party headquarters at 447 Westminster Street, Providence, around midday on September 13. Police seized a truck containing more than a ton of paraphernalia and pamphlets, including 1000 copies of *The Daily Worker*. Six people were immediately taken into custody and a dozen more arrested later that day, including Lawrence Spitz, one of the men who disrupted the Labor Day speeches earlier in the month. According to police, the "reds" were organizing a march on the State House because inside the office on Westminster Street they found a mimeograph machine and thousands of flyers with the following message printed on them:

Fellow workers: Today at the state legislature, the General Assembly is called into special session by Governor Green, who will ask for $100,000 to increase the State Police force to 500. NOT ENOUGH BLOOD is on the governor's hands yet - he wants more forces with which to attack the workers. TODAY- the workers must give their answer to the outrageous criminal shootings. TODAY - we must make the mill owners' agents who sit in the State House respect the workers' right their usual MASS PICKETS. On this depends the success or failure of the strike. This is a matter of bread and butter - OF LIFE AND DEATH. [202]

Upon hearing the news of the arrests, Sylvia issued a public statement on behalf of the UTW:

After receiving reports from field workers who were on the scene in both Saylesville and Woonsocket last night, when serious uprisings occurred, resulting in one man being slain and many wounded, the Rhode Island strike committee today went on record advising workers not to tolerate or have anything to do with communists who have invaded the Blackstone Valley strike area. Reports from these same field workers have convinced us that communists imported into the strike area from New York, Boston, Lawrence, and Providence were solely responsible for the uprisings that took place both in Saylesville and Woonsocket.

Communists, known for their extreme radical tendencies, and including some of the prominent leaders of that group, were active in both the Central Falls and Woonsocket disorders. It is our intention as members of the Rhode Island Strike Committee that the strike will continue in a peaceful manner, and, towards this end, we urge all members of the United Textile Workers of American to rid themselves of communists and their activities.[203]

In response to the raids, the Communist Party-affiliated International Labor Defense sent a telegram to the General Assembly, demanding Governor Green be impeached for using the raids to stifle the rights of workers to organize and for ordering "cold-blooded shooting, clubbing, wounding and gassing of hundreds of these workers by National Guards, and has deputized gun-thugs."[204] There is no record of the telegram even being received, never mind read, by any member of the Assembly. Of all of those arrested during the roundup, only one person, Irving Kaitz, admitted to being present in the Saylesville area, and he claimed his involvement was limited to throwing fourteen rocks in one of the melees. At the trial for the arrested communists on October 2, prosecutors presented no evidence any of the other arrestees were involved in the strike disturbances. Only Kaitz was convicted on a riot charge while the others were convicted of petty crimes such as vagrancy.[205]

With the shutdown of the Saylesville mill, the closing of the chaotic special session of the General Assembly, and a roundup of suspected "reds," Sylvia called a meeting of UTW leaders to discuss next steps. The meeting took place at 9:00 Friday evening at the UTW union hall at 23 Broad Street in Pawtucket. The group was smaller than usual, which is probably why it took place here instead of at the general strike headquarters at the Labor Temple. Despite purportedly being a "secret" meeting, the press was waiting for Sylvia to arrive. He told reporters: "we have made enough headway here so that there's nothing to amount to anything in operation in Rhode Island. The State is tied up. And it will remain tied up until the mills settle with us."

THE AFTERMATH

The following Sunday, September 16, Charles Gorcynski was buried in Notre Dame Cemetery. Thousands of people marched behind the funeral cortege following services at St. James Polish Catholic Church in Central Falls. The quiet on the streets of Saylesville held while the mill remained closed. But if Sylvia's claims that the mills were "tied up" it was surely with loose bonds, because on September 18, the Saylesville plant announced it would be reopening.[206] By agreement between the UTW and the governor, picketing was allowed at the facility, but the union was limited to having only 140 people on the lines at any time. They divided their numbers into seven groups of twenty, and they paraded in front of the facility, from Walker Street to Smithfield Ave. Although some employees of the bleachery reported their houses were hit with rocks the night before the re-opening of the facility, there were no disturbances at the bleachery itself and nearly all the Sayles workforce reported for duty as scheduled.[207]

As other mills across Rhode Island began to resume operations, a commission appointed by President Roosevelt prepared to release a report on the national strike. A three-person commission, originally appointed by the President on September 5, was chaired by former Republican governor of New Hampshire John Winant. The Winant Commission originally tried to arbitrate the dispute after Gorman made that recommendation on September 8. Sloan from the textile employers group rejected the idea outright on September 9; so Winant instead investigated the UTW's claims about poor working conditions in the industry.[208]

On September 20, the commission released its findings.

President Roosevelt said "The excellent report of the Board of Inquiry for the cotton textile industry presents findings and recommendations which cover the basic sources of difficulties, and does this in a way which shows the wholly fair and reasonable approach which the board undertook its task."[209] He then urged an end to the strike, saying " I want to express the very sincere hope that all employees now on strike will return to work and that all textile manufacturers will aid the government in carrying out the steps outlined," in the Winant Commission's report.[210]

Among the commission's recommendations were a directive to the Federal Department of Labor to do a statistical analysis of the union's claims about poor working conditions and a directive to the Federal Trade Commission to investigate the economic status of the industry. The Commission then directed the agencies to report their findings to the President so he could make recommendations for wage adjustments for the workers.[211] Winant's report also made it clear the textile employers refused to arbitrate the dispute even though the union was willing to do so. The report was also critical of the textile industry's self-appointed NRA Code enforcement committee. The report cited them for creating "widespread dissatisfaction" by using management representatives to investigate complaints by labor against management which "cannot be defended from any standpoint consistent with the principles upon which the Recovery Act is founded."[212]

UTW leader Francis Gorman was elated with the report, considering it a complete vindication of the union's decision to strike. Gorman told reporters:

By the President's order a copy of the report of the Winant board was presented to us tonight at the same hour the report was given to the newspapers. It is impossible to digest in a few moments the contents of a report so voluminous. My only comment at this time is that so far as I now understand the report, it is an indictment of management and indicates that the position of the union has been right.[213]

When asked if this meant the strike was over, Gorman answered: "Until the executive council decides otherwise the strike will and must continue in full force." He then announced he was calling the executive council together immediately to consider whether to call off the strike.[214]

On September 22, the members of the UTW executive council met at union headquarters in Washington, DC, and formally voted to end the strike. AFL President William Green, who attended the executive council meeting, told reporters "It's a victory for the workers. The position of the textile workers has been completely vindicated." Strike leader Gorman, reporting the vote to end the strike was voted unanimously by the executive council, declared "our strike has torn apart the whole unjust structure of (the) NRA." He telegraphed every local union in the country, announcing "your heroic strike ends in complete victory."[215]

The textile industry received the report with a shrug. George Sloan announced the industry group would give the Winant Commission's report "serious consideration", but they never formally acted on any of its recommendations.[216] Across the country, workers took down their picket lines and began the process of reporting to work to restart the mills.

In Rhode Island, plants not yet open began reactivating and workers reporting for work. At the Saylesville bleachery, management compiled lists of those arrested in the disturbances, thirty-seven people in total. The list includes the arrestee's names, ages, gender, and addresses. Whether or not this list was to serve as a "blacklist" - workers not to be employed by the facility - is unclear.[217] While some minor jousting between the union and employers about who should be reporting to work and when surfaced, the process generally proceeded without major controversy.

On October 6, the Rhode Island AFL met in Newport, Rhode Island, for its annual convention. The delegates were greeted by Mayor Mortimer Sullivan and apart from a delayed start as delegates made their way from across the state to Newport, the convention got underway with high spirits. However, a controversy erupted on the first day when Rob Hill, a delegate from Carpenters Local 94, submitted to the resolutions committee a resolution condemning Governor Green for his actions during the strike. Hill took to the floor after formally submitting the resolution, reading it along with a statement to the convention:

As always when troops are used for police duty, lives were lost and many people were injured. Had the strikers been allowed to picket the mills, as is their right, the necessity for calling the troops would not have occurred. It was the refusal of those in control to allow the strikers to picket the plants that caused the trouble. As proof of this, no disturbance of any consequence took place after this right was recognized. Charging that the disturbance was caused by communists, the governor copying the methods of the dictators of Europe, issued an order calling for the arrest of all known communists. According to the report in the press, 17 persons were arrested but the charge of rioting was placed against one person only. The others were charged with being idle persons. The police were unable to get sufficient evidence to connect them to the strike. The governor is a candidate for re-election next November, but should be retired to private life for his actions during the strike, Therefore, be it:

Resolved - WE, the delegates to the semi-annual convention of the Rhode Island State Branch of the American Federation of Labor, call upon all workers of the State to vote against the re-election of Governor Theodore Francis Green as Governor of the State of Rhode Island.[218]

Green's election was scheduled for the next month, November 1934. After Hill's speech, the UTW's McMahon addressed the delegates. He thanked them for their support in the strike, especially for their financial support, which he assured them the money was well spent. Joseph Sylvia then took to the floor and told the delegates he placed no blame on Governor Green for what took place in the streets of Saylesville. Instead, he placed the blame squarely on the shoulders of Sheriff Andrews for unleashing his deputy sheriffs on the picketers. Unbelievably, he told the audience that Governor Green was not responsible for calling out the Guard and the picket lines had been peaceful until "political powers of the state" had sent the sheriffs to the mills.[219]

The next day, the delegates debated Hill's resolution for over two hours. Hill spoke in favor, as did a delegate named Ganz, representing the Newport Machinists' local union. Ganz focused his argument on the governor's round up of alleged communists, telling the audience "I am not a communist, but I respect their right to their opinions. Green had no more right to order their arrest than to order the arrest of all labor leaders." State AFL President William Connolly spoke against the resolution from the floor, reminding the convention that the UTW leaders McMahon and Sylvia both praised Governor Green for his actions during the strike. In a moment of *realpolitik*, Connolly told the body, "If we pass this resolution, where are we going to get off going to the State House for legislation with a Republican governor?"[220]

Hill's resolution failed and the convention voted to endorse Governor Green's re-election. Governor Green was then introduced to address the convention. He praised the Rhode Island labor movement for bringing forth labor leaders like McMahon and Gorman. He told the delegates he heard no criticism of the State Police or the National Guard during the strike but heard plenty of complaints against the deputy sheriffs and said Andrews took his orders not from him, but from the manufacturers. Green said:

Two years ago, I included your entire 11 suggestions in my party platform and introduced bills in the legislature in their favor. If a more liberal instead of reactionary group were in control of our state senate they would have passed. I am proud of our Rhode Island labor and its leaders, who have become national figures, such as Thomas McMahon and Francis A.

Gorman ...You have the answer in your power, the ballot box. In closing I again assure you of my cooperation and will welcome your suggestions.[221]

The convention did pass a resolution calling for a ban on the use of the National Guard for use in labor strikes except in case of rioting or revolt. They also passed a resolution against "communistic disorders" and called for a committee of labor leaders to collect data on all communistic organizations and their activities. Prior to adjourning the convention also passed resolutions against the organizing of workers along industrial lines in favor of the traditional craft union structure, and a resolution instructing the executive council to consider organizing women teachers into a unit of the American Federation of Teachers.[222]

William Blackwood died of his wounds the day after the convention. His funeral took place at the First Baptist Church in Pawtucket the following Thursday, and he was buried in the Ballou Cemetery in Cumberland, Rhode Island.[223] There is no record that the UTW acknowledged his passing and his grave, to this day, is unmarked.

With the endorsement of organized labor secured, Governor Green campaigned as Roosevelt's man in Rhode Island. His opponent, Republican State Senator Luke Callan, tried to paint the governor as a coward for calling out the National Guard during the strike, but the message did not resonate with Rhode Island voters. On election day, November 6, Governor Green was re-elected with fifty-seven percent of the vote. [224]

Governor Green was scheduled to be inaugurated on January 1, 1935, but party control of the Rhode Island General Assembly remained unresolved because the vote counts in three senate districts were contested, with some alleging fraud. In what came to be known as the "Bloodless Revolution," on inauguration day, Green and other Democratic Party leaders orchestrated, through a series of questionable maneuvers, for the Democratic Party candidates to be declared the victors in each of the contested districts, giving the Democratic Party total control over the General Assembly. Before the end of the day, the Rhode Island Supreme Court was replaced, and the Republican Party controlled offices of High Sheriff, Providence Safety Board, and Finance Commissioner eliminated. The Democratic Party established complete hegemony over the levers of power in the state.[225]

CONCLUSION

The chapter in Richard Kelley's book *Nine Lives For Labor* about the 1934 textiles strike is called "The Union That Wasn't There." In this chapter, Kelly describes a worried Thomas McMahon being driven from a pre-strike meeting repeatedly muttering under his breath "a million mouths to feed." Faced with the seemingly impossible task of leading a nationwide strike with a union that in recent months didn't even have enough printed membership cards to sign up all of the workers who wished to join, the unrealistic expectations of the members of the union undoubtedly caused McMahon to shudder. [226]

Both nationally and in Rhode Island, the national textile strike of 1934 was a failure. The union was completely unprepared to lead an operation on this scale and it never should have called the strike. From the end of the UTW convention in New York City in August 1934, through the duration of the strike, the operation lurched from crisis to crisis. This was especially true in Rhode Island. In the UTW's defense, it is not surprising things would be chaotic given the context of a national strike in an industry with less than complete union membership density. But even with the pre-strike attention, most workers did not immediately answer the call to walk off their jobs in Rhode Island. The first week of the strike evolved slowly, and even if we discount both the owners claims of continued operating capacity and the union's counter claims of strike effectiveness, by the time Saylesville erupted it is probable as many as half of the textile workers in the state were still tending their machines.

The UTW's command of the situation in Rhode Island was challenged in other significant ways. Though they won the support of the local AFL early on, other independent textile unions either ignored or reluctantly delayed the call to join the strike. Sylvia had to explain to workers, seemingly through the management slanted press, that when the UTW called for the strike of all textile workers, it meant in all the connected industries, including bleacheries. The workers in those connected mills, most of whom were not UTW members, did not receive the message in the way it was intended, if at all. On the picket lines in Saylesville and elsewhere, the UTW had little control over the people engaged in either rioting or picketing, were ignored by the police and the people, and in many cases tried to distance themselves from the actual events on the streets.

Given the UTW's inept leadership of the strike in Rhode Island, it is highly questionable what happened in Saylesville was because the UTW specifically targeted that bleachery for closure. When the first pickets arrived at the Saylesville bleachery on September 7, three days after the strike began, the plant was not the only bleachery in the state still operating. While some bleacheries did close, several others were still open, including the nearby Lincoln Bleachery and Dye Works of Lonsdale. The Lonsdale operation was not as large as its neighbor in Saylesville, but with 600 workers, it was no small outfit. Once the violence erupted in Saylesville local media turned their attention away from a running tally of what shops were open versus those that were closed; so, it is unclear what happened next with the other bleacheries. But despite the company's insistence they were being targeted, a notion adopted by Findlay and Salmond, it seems more coincidence than intentional.

It is also clear Governor Green bumbled his way through the strike. He changed his message about the strike on several occasions as he cast about for someone to blame for the violence, switching from blaming the reactionaries, who did seem to have a role to play in the violence, to the communists, who did not. The men under his authority did their best to ignore him and the elected members of the General Assembly undercut his authority. It was only by making common cause with the UTW and the labor movement after the strike was over placing the blame on "communists" that Green's reputation was spared.

This event was not a "communist uprising." The record clearly demonstrates even if certain members of the Communist Party were present on the streets of Saylesville, they played no leadership role whatsoever in the action. Only one member of the Community Party was ever charged in connection to the disorder. The raid at the party headquarters on Westminster Street on September 13 is comically anti-climactic, happening when the communists were planning a rally to protect the workers after the shooting stopped. As Secretary of War Dern said to reporters when he was asked about the so-called communist uprising, "you must realize it's a custom now to blame the communists for a lot of things."[227]

Likewise, it is clear the uprising in the streets was not caused by "outsiders." If you recall, UTW leaders like Sylvia pleaded with Governor Green not to impose picketing restrictions, that they could operate the picket lines peacefully, and that any trouble in Rhode Island was imported from other states. The facts, however, make clear the vast majority involved on the streets were local people from the surrounding area. One person from Connecticut was arrested during the disturbances in Saylesville, a few from the Boston area, but nearly everyone else caught and charged by the police lived within walking distance of the Saylesville bleachery. Similarly, according to the list of casualties, most of their addresses are from the working class neighborhoods of Central Falls and Pawtucket.

Recall also how on the first day of violence in Saylesville, the UTW men who were there, Brunelle and Powers, tried to keep a group of you boys from throwing rocks at the plant and the sheriffs. In her interview with the University of Rhode Island's *Mill Worker Oral History Project* of the mid 1970's, local resident Rachel Landry told interviewers, when asked who was involved with the violence that it was "young fellas, I guess."[228] When Rita Brouillette, the 16-year-old girl from nearby Etna Street in Central Falls, was arrested by police, a wire service headline read "Just Having

Fun Arrested Rioters Declare."[229] A sensationalized headline for sure, but not far from the mark.

What I believed happened on the streets of Saylesville was neighborhood riot caused by armed thugs provoking local youths into doing something foolish, which then escalated to the point of civil disorder. Following the timeline of events on September 7 through 12, the flow of the action shows most of the violence started between the hours of 2:00 and 3:00 in the afternoon, just as local schools released students, lulled around dinner time, and then resumed in the evening hours of late summer when the sun was still out and temperatures still warm. The action attracted curiosity seekers, many of whom were likely strike-idled area workers, swelling the size of the crowd providing cover for young people to keep the fight against the sheriffs going.

The political establishment used the violence on the streets to stake out positions serving their own needs, ascribing intentions fitting their own conclusions, and when the action was over, created narratives to protect themselves. Governor Green, mindful of how one of his predecessors lost re-election for mishandling a textile strike, seized the opportunity to take credit for the end of the violence. The Rhode Island labor movement, ascendent with newfound allies in the early days of the New Deal, joined forces with Green and helped share his version of the story, complete with communist bogeymen.

For further evidence for how quickly the people involved tried to bury the story of the Saylesville Massacre, on January 30, 1935, the political establishment in Rhode Island held a Gala Ball to celebrate FDR's birthday at the Exchange Street Armory in Providence, one of the mustering cites for the National Guard on their way to Saylesville. UTW organizer Stella Moskwa was escorted to the event by Rhode Island's Lt. Governor Robert Quinn and crowned "Queen of the Ball" by Democratic Party Boss Tom McCoy.[230] The Democratic Party had much to celebrate. In addition to surviving the strike, thanks to the maneuvering of McCoy and Green, the Democratic Party took complete control of the political order in Rhode Island. Green and McCoy's coup in January of

1935 has come down to us known as the "Bloodless Revolution" only because it was convenient to all involved to forget as quickly as possible the bloody deaths of Charles Gorcynski and William Blackwood.

BIBLIOGRAPHY

Aitken, Hugh G.J. *Scientific Management in Action: Taylorism at Watertown Arsenal, 1908-1915*. Princeton, Princeton University Press, 2014.

Alford, L. P. *Henry Laurence Gantt: Leader in Industry*. 1st ed. New York, New York: The American Society of Mechanical Engineers, 1934.

Bayles, Richard Mather. *History of Providence County, Rhode Island*. 2nd ed. New York: W. W. Preston, 1891. http://archive.org/details/historyofprovide02inbayl.

Bernstein, Irving. *The Turbulent Years: A History of the American Worker, 1933-1940*. Chicago, Illinois: Haymarket Books, 2010.

Bogren, George G., "Treatment of Cotton Finishing Wastes at the Sayles Finishing Plants, Inc." *Sewage and Industrial Wastes* 24, no. 8 (Aug 1, 1952): 994-1000. http://www.jstor.org/stable/25031939.

Brecher, Jeremy. *Strike!* Revised and updated ed. Boston, Massachusetts: South End Press, 1997.

Brooks, Robert R. *When Labor Organizes*. New Haven: Yale Univ. Press, 1938.

Browder, Dorothea. "Elizabeth Nord's Tennis Lesson: How a Labor Leader Got Her Start in the Pawtucket-Central Falls YWCA Industrial Program." *Rhode Island History* 71, no. 2 (Summer/Fall, 2013): 56-80.

Brown Alumni Monthly, Vol. XXV, No. 4, (Providence, Rhode Island), November 1934. http://archive.org/details/brownalumnimonth1134brow.

Buhle, Paul, M., ed. *Working Lives: An Oral History of Rhode Island Labor*. Providence, Rhode Island, The Rhode Island Historical Society, 1987.

Cohen, Lizabeth. *Making a New Deal: Industrial Workers in Chicago, 1919-1939*. Repr. ed. Cambridge: Univ. Press, 1996.

Commission to Investigate Problems of the Cotton Textile Industry. Providence, Rhode Island: The Oxford Press, 1935.

Daniel, Cletus E. *Culture of Misfortune: An Interpretive History of Textile Unionism in the United States*. Ithaca: ILR Press, 2001.

Dresser, Robert B., "The Case for Tax Relief", *The Freeman* (Orange, Connecticut), Vol. 5, No. 3, September 1954.

Dresser, Robert B., "Statement of Robert B. Dresser," *Committee for Constitutional Government* (New York, New York), undated. https://history.fee.org/publications/statement-of-robert-b-dresser/

Dunnigan, Kate and Richard Quinney. "Work and Community in Saylesville." *Radical History Review* 17, (Apr 1, 1978): 173. https://search.proquest.com/docview/1295932825.

Engelberg, Eliza S. ""What is a Home without Money and Food?": Working Women's Identity and the Rhode Island Textile Mill Strike of 1922," master's thesis, Brown University, 1991.

Faue, Elizabeth. *Community of Suffering & Struggle: Women, Men, and the Labor Movement in Minneapolis, 1915-1945*. Gender & American Culture. Chapel Hill: University of North Carolina, 1991. http://catalog.hathitrust.org/Record/002467989.

Findlay, James "The Great Textile Strike of 1934: Illuminating Rhode Island History in the Thirties." *Rhode Island History* 42, no. 1, February 1, 1983).

Foner, Philip Sheldon. *Women and the American Labor Movement*. New York, New York, Free Press, 1982.

Gerstle, Gary. *Working-Class Americanism: The Politics of Labor in a Textile City, 1914-1960*. Princeton and Oxford: Princeton University Press, 2002.

Goodman, Jay S. *Changes in the Old Alliance: The Democrats and Labor in Rhode Island 1952-1962*. Providence, Rhode Island: Brown University Press, 1967.

Gordon, A.J., "Rhode Island Legislators Balk Move for U.S. Troops; Governor Sees Red Revolt," September 14, 1934. https://search.proquest.com/docview/100977873.

Hadcock, Editha. "Labor Problems in the Rhode Island Cotton Mills." *Rhode Island History* 14, no. 3 (Jul 1, 1955a): 82. http://www.rihs.org/assetts/files/publications/1955_July.pdf.

Hadcock, Editha " Labor Problems in the Rhode Island Cotton Mills [Concluded from July, 1955, V. 14, no. 3, Page 93]." *Rhode Island History* 14, no. 4 (Oct 1, 1955b): 110. http://www.rihs.org/assetts/files/publications/1955_Oct.pdf.

Hall, Joseph Davis. *Biographical History of the Manufacturers and Business Men of Rhode Island, at the Opening of the Twentieth Century*. Providence, R.I., J. D. Hall & co., 1901. http://archive.org/details/biographicalhist00hall.

Harris, John, "Roosevelt Pleased Troops Not Needed: Secretary Dern Reveals 4000 Held Ready," *The Daily Boston Globe*, September 16, 1934.

Hathaway, C. A. *Communists in the Textile Strike: An Answer to Gorman, Green and Co.* New York, New York: Central Committee of the Communist Party U.S.A., 1934.

Hughes, Quenby Olmsted. "Red Flame Burning Bright: Communist Labor Organizer Ann Burlak, Rhode Island Workers, and the New Deal." *Rhode Island History* 67, no. 2 (Summer/Fall, 2009): 43-60.

"Introduction - Moshassuck Valley Railroad," Accessed Feb 16, 2018. https://sites.google.com/site/moshassuckvalleyrailroad/Home/introduction-1.

Irons, Janet Christine. *Testing the New Deal: The General Textile Strike on 1934 in the American South*. Urbana and Chicago: University of Illinois Press, 2000.

Jaffe, Susan E. "Ethnic Working Class Protest: The Textile Strike of 1922 in Rhode Island," master's thesis, Brown University, 1974.

Kelly, Richard. *Nine Lives for Labor*. New York: Frederick A. Praeger, Inc., 1956.

Lamphere, Louise. *From Working Daughters to Working Mothers: Immigrant Women in a New England Industrial Community*. Ithaca and London: Cornell University Press, 1987.

Laxton, Mildred. *Saylesville*. Lincoln, Rhode Island: Lincoln Public Library.

Levine, Erwin L. *Theodore Francis Green: The Rhode Island Years, 1906-1936*. Providence, Rhode Island: Brown University Press, 1963.

Luff, Jennifer. *Commonsense Anticommunism*. Chapel Hill: The University of North Carolina Press, 2012.

MacLoughlin, William Gerald. *Rhode Island: A History*. New York, New York: W.W. Norton & Company, 1978.

Marsh, J. T. *An Introduction to Textile Bleaching*. New York: J. Wiley & Sons, 1948. https://catalog.hathitrust.org/Record/005947287.

McMahon, Thomas. "The Textile Situation." *Vital Speeches of the Day* (October 22, 1934): 53-54.

Meyers, Adena. "Rhode Island Women Activists in the 1934 General Textile Strike." In *Working in the Blackstone River Valley: Exploring the Heritage of Industrialization*, edited by Reynolds, Douglas M. and Marjory Myers, 165-175. Woonsocket, Rhode Island: Rhode Island Labor History Society, 1991.

Rhode Island Adjutant General's Report Relative to Strike Duty in 1934. Providence, Rhode Island, Rhode Island Secretary of State, 1934.

Sachs, Lynn. *American Labor Discontent and the Rise of Unionism: Focus on the Textile Strike of 1934, Saylesville, Rhode Island*. Providence, Rhode Island: Rhode Island Historical Society, 1981.

Salmond, John A. *The General Textile Strike of 1934: From Maine to Alabama*. Columbia: University of Missouri Press, 2002.

Sayles Finishing Plants (Saylesville, Phillipsdale, and Valley Falls, Rhode Island, and Asheville, North Carolina) Business Records 1906 - 1971, The Sayles Finishing Plant Ephemera collection (MSS 6, sg 35), Rhode Island Historical Society, Manuscripts Division, Providence, Rhode Island.

Smith, Mathew J., "The Real McCoy," *Rhode Island History* (Providence, Rhode Island), Vol. 32, Number 3, August 1973.

Soule, George. "Class War in Rhode Island." *The New Republic* (August 5, 1931): 308-312.

Stabler, Herman and Pratt, Gilbert H. *The Purification of some Textile and Other Factory Wastes*. Washington, DC.: Department of the Interior, United States Geological Survey, 1909.

Stark, Louis, "Board Drops Move for Arbitration." *The New York Times*, September 13, 1934. https://search.proquest.com/docview/101230952.

Sterba, Christopher M. "Family, Work, and Nation: Hazelton, Pennsylvania, and the 1934 General Strike in Textiles." 120, no. 1/2 (Jan 1, 1996): 3-35. http://ojs.libraries.psu.edu/index.php/pmhb/article/view/45055.

Stern, Boris. "Productivity of Labor and Industry: Mechanical Changes in the Cotton-Textile Industry, 1910 to 1936." *Monthly Labor Review* 45, no. 2 (August 1937): 316-343. https://www.jstor.org/stable/41815211.

Survey Report African American Struggle for Civil Rights in Rhode Island: The Twentieth Century, RI Historical Preservation and Heritage Commission (Providence, Rhode Island), July 2, 2019.

The Boston Daily Globe. "Riot at Saylesville, RI, As Night Shift Leaves," September 8, 1934.

The Boston Daily Globe. "Saylesville Hands Return," November 18, 1905.

The Boston Daily Globe. "Saylesville Armed Camp," September 11,

1934.

The Coast Artillery Journal. "States Uses of the National Guard," v.78, no. 2, March-April, 1935.

The Indiana Gazette. ""Just having Fun" Arrested Rioters Declare," September 13, 1934. https://www.newspapers.com/clip/282616/the_indiana_gazette/.

The Militant. "Mill Workers Slain by Guards; Governor Raises "Red" Scare," September 15, 1934.

The New Republic. "Textile Trouble," September 19, 1934.

The New Republic. "Two Sides of the Barricades," October 10, 1934.

The New York Times. "Guard Called Out in New England," September 11, 1934.

The New York Times. "3,000 Fight Troops in Rhode Island," September 12, 1934.

The New York Times. "Rhode Island Governor Issues Proclamation," September 13, 1934.

The New York Times. "Strike is Praised by Norman Thomas," September 13, 1934.

The New York Times. "5000 Troops Out in New England," September 16, 1934.

The New York Times. "More Mills Close in New England," September 19, 1934.

The New York Times. "Winant Board Asks for End of Strike with Jobs Assured," September 21, 1934.

The New York Times. "Robert B. Dresser, Lawyer and Conservative Spokesman," September 26, 1976.

The News. "Labor Branch Blocks Rebuke to Governor," (Newport, Rhode Island), October 8, 1934.

The Pawtucket Times. "Sidelights of Strike," September 11, 1934.

The Pawtucket Times. "2 Badly Wounded by Trapped Troops in Cemetery Area," September 12, 1934.

The Pawtucket Times. "Green Asks Public to Assist in Bringing

Order in Saylesville," September 12, 1934.

The Pawtucket Times. "Sidelights of Strike," September 12, 1934.

The Pawtucket Times. "8 'Red' Suspects Captured in Raid," September 13, 1934.

The Pawtucket Times. "Reds Fomenting Mill Strike, Providence Police Convinced," September 13, 1934.

The Pawtucket Times. "Rioters Beat Truck Driver," September 13, 1934.

The Pawtucket Times. "Text of Letter to Governor in Closing of Sayles Mill," September 13, 1934.

The Providence Journal. "Cotton Textile Strike Is Voted," August 17, 1934.

The Providence Journal. "Textile Leader Will Set Up Headquarters," August 21, 1934.

The Providence Journal. "U.T.W. Council to Meet Here Saturday Afternoon," August 22, 1934.

The Providence Journal. "Organizer Denies Sept. 4 Date Set," August 27, 1934.

The Providence Journal. "Joseph Sylvia Hurt in Motor Accident," August 29, 1934.

The Providence Journal. "Green Declares Strike Justified," August 30, 1934.

The Providence Journal. "Cotton Textile Strike Called for Tomorrow Night; 11th Hour Conference is Failure," August 31, 1934.

The Providence Journal. "Employers Say Few Will Strike," September 1, 1934.

The Providence Journal. "R.I. Textile Mills Open to Workers Tuesday Morning," September 1, 1934.

The Providence Journal. "Strike Leader Announces Plan to Picket Mill," September 1, 1934.

The Providence Journal. "Wool Unions Get Walkout Order," September 1, 1934.

The Providence Journal. "Most Employers in State Assert Few Will Strike," September 2, 1934.

The Providence Journal. "Sloan Calls Union Demands Preposterous and Ruinous," September 2, 1934.

The Providence Journal. "Leader Says Strike to Go on in Spite of "Hell, High Water"," September 3, 1934.

The Providence Journal. "McMahon Makes Appeal to Labor," September 4, 1934.

The Providence Journal. "Conditions in Rhode Island Textile Plants as Disclosed by Survey," September 5, 1934.

The Providence Journal. "Only 19 Plants Close in State, 100 Unaffected," September 5, 1934.

The Providence Journal. "16,000 Workers Out of Plants in Rhode Island," September 6, 1934.

The Providence Journal. "Mill Men Ask Governor to Protect those Who Want to Work," September 6, 1934.

The Providence Journal. "Green Asks all to Remain Calm," September 7, 1934.

The Providence Journal. "Sheriff Prohibits further Picketing at Saylesville; Weekend Quit Prevails," September 8, 1934.

The Providence Journal. "State Troopers Drive 2000 from Big Sayles Mill," September 8, 1934.

The Providence Journal. "State Troopers Rout Mob of 2000 Strikers After Disorder at Saylesville Plant," September 8, 1934.

The Providence Journal. "Troy and Bodwell Clash Over Strike," September 8, 1934.

The Providence Journal. "Woonsocket Men Vote to Strike," September 9, 1934.

The Providence Journal. "1500 at Strike Meeting in Pawtuxet Valley," September 10, 1934.

The Providence Journal. "Police Act to Stop Intimidation of Mill Workers in Providence," September 10, 1934.

The Providence Journal. "R.I. Mills Renew Resistance Today," September 10, 1934.

The Providence Journal. "Bayonets Hold Back Sayles Plant Mobs," September 11, 1934.

The Providence Journal. "Green Orders Guardsmen Mobilized for Strike Duty; 3 Shot at Saylesville," September 11, 1934.

The Providence Journal. "Governor Issues Call on Appeal of High Sheriff," September 11, 1934.

The Providence Journal. "Guardsmen Go into Action with Sticks - Strikers Fight, but Retreat," September 11, 1934.

The Providence Journal. "The Saylesville Riot," September 11, 1934.

The Providence Journal. "Coats Employes (sic) Call on Governor to Protect Them," September 12, 1934.

The Providence Journal. "Governor Explains Troop Call; Says Gunfire Caused Decision," September 12, 1934.

The Providence Journal. "Keep Politics Out of the Strike," September 12, 1934.

The Providence Journal. "Seven National Guards among Injured at Saylesville," September 12, 1934.

The Providence Journal. "Soldiers, Driven Back by Rocks, Fire and Charge with Fixed Bayonets," September 12, 1934.

The Providence Journal. "Subversive Radical Influence is Evident in State, Police Say," September 12, 1934.

The Providence Journal. "Green Announces Pact to Limit Number of Sayles Plant Pickets," September 13, 1934.

The Providence Journal. "Sayles Plant Will Close at Request of Governor," September 13, 1934.

The Providence Journal. "Three of Mob Dying in Sayles Mill Riot," September 13, 1934.

The Providence Journal. "15 Communists Arrested in Drive Throughout City," September 14, 1934.

The Providence Journal. "Governor Green Asks Assembly for Power to Call in Federal Troops to Quell "Communist Uprising" " September 14, 1934.

The Providence Journal. "None of Green's Plans to Meet Crisis Adopted," September 14, 1934.

The Providence Journal. "Quiet Prevails in Strike Area," September 14, 1934.

The Providence Journal. "Call to Prayer on Textile Strike," September 15, 1934.

The Providence Journal. "Green's Strike Program Killed by Adjournment," September 15, 1934.

The Providence Journal. "Sloan Denounces Flying Squadrons," September 15, 1934.

The Providence Journal. "Labor Defense Demands Impeachment of Green," September 16, 1934.

The Providence Journal. "Sayles Finishing Co. Plant Will Open Tomorrow," September 18, 1934.

The Providence Journal. "Finishing Plant at Saylesville to Reopen Today," September 19, 1934.

The Providence Journal. "1100 Employes (sic) Return to Jobs at Saylesville," September 20, 1934.

The Providence Journal. "Roosevelt Approves Winant Body Plan," September 21, 1934.

The Providence Journal. "Mill Hands Ordered to Return Tomorrow," September 23, 1934.

The Providence Journal. "8 Alleged 'Reds' Appear on Trial," October 3, 1934.

The Providence Journal. "A.F.L. Resolution Scores Governor," October 7, 1934.

The Providence Journal. "R.I. Labor Fails to Rebuke Green," October 8, 1934.

The Providence Journal. "Rites Thursday for Strike Victim," October 9, 1934.

The Providence Sunday Journal, "Many Pawtucket Society Folk Enjoying Southern Sojourns," February 3, 1935.

The Washington Post. "'Girl in Green' Leads New Riot, Hunted in R.I. Fatal Outbreak," September 16, 1934.

The Woonsocket Call. "R.I. Operatives Will Act Tomorrow On Decision Of Textile Unions To Strike," August 18, 1934.

Transcript of Interview with Elizabeth Nord. *Mill Life Oral History Collection.*, edited by Kantor, Harvey & Findlay, James. Box 28 ed. Vol. Folder 58. South Kingstown, Rhode Island: University of Rhode Island, 1975a.

Transcript of Interview with Elliot Broadbent. *Mill Life Oral History Collection.*, edited by Kantor, Harvey & Findlay, James. Box 29 ed. Vol. Folders 81-83. South Kingstown, Rhode Island: University of Rhode Island, 1973.

Transcript of Interview with Harold Fletcher. *Mill Life Oral History Collection.*, edited by Kantor, Harvey & Findlay, James. Box 25 ed. Vol. Folder 36. South Kingstown, Rhode Island: University of Rhode Island, 1974.

Transcript of Interview with Rachel Landry. *Mill Life Oral History Collection.*, edited by Kantor, Harvey & Findlay, James. Box 27 ed. Vol. Folder 56. South Kingstown, Rhode Island: University of Rhode Island, 1975b.

Turner, Bruce. "The Textile Industry and Organized Labor in Rhode Island, 1920-1940, " master's thesis, University of Rhode Island, 1959.

[1] John A. Salmond, *The General Textile Strike of 1934: From Maine to Alabama* (Columbia: University of Missouri Press, 2002), x.

[2] Quinnville, Limerock, Fairlawn, Manville, and Albion are the others.

[3] Mildred Laxton, *Saylesville* (Lincoln, Rhode Island: Lincoln Public Library), undated.

[4] J. T. Marsh, *An Introduction to Textile Bleaching* (New York: J. Wiley & Sons, 1948). https://catalog.hathitrust.org/Record/005947287 , viii.

[5] Ibid.

[6] Stabler, Herman and Pratt, Gilbert H., *The Purification of some Textile and Other Factory Wastes* (Washington, DC.: Department of the Interior, United States Geological Survey, [1909]), 27-29.

[7] L. P. Alford, *Henry Laurence Gantt: Leader in Industry*, 1st ed. (New York, New York: The American Society of Mechanical Engineers, 1934).

[8] Hugh G.J. Aitken, *Scientific Management in Action: Taylorism at Watertown Arsenal, 1908-1915*. Course Book ed., Princeton: Princeton University Press, 2014. muse.jhu.edu/book/34265.

[9] No author, "untitled," *American Wool and Cotton Reporter*, Vol. XIX, No. 45, (Boston, New York, & Philadelphia), November 16, 1905, 9. "Saylesville Hands Return." *The Boston Daily Globe*, November 18, 1905.

[10] J Susan E. Jaffe "Ethnic Working Class Protest: The Textile Strike of 1922 in Rhode Island," (master's thesis, Brown University, 1974.)

[11] Irving Bernstein, *The Turbulent Years: A History of the American Worker, 1933-1940* (Chicago, Illinois: Haymarket Books, 2010). Janet Christine Irons, *Testing the New Deal: The General Textile Strike of 1934 in the American South* (Urbana and Chicago: University of Illinois Press, 2000). Cletus E. Daniel, *Culture of Misfortune: An Interpretive History of Textile Unionism in the United States* (Ithaca: ILR Press, 2001).
John A. Salmond, *The General Textile Strike of 1934: From Maine to Alabama* (Columbia: University of Missouri Press, 2002).

[12] Bernstein, 34.

[13] Bernstein, 35 and 217.

[14] Daniels, 40.

[15] Ibid., 33. Daniel attributes this quotation to Socialist leader Norman Thomas.

[16] Richard Kelley, *Nine Lives For Labor* (New York, Frederick A. Praeger, Inc, 1956), 65.

[17] Lizabeth Cohen, *Making a New Deal: Industrial Workers in Chicago, 1919-1939*, Repr. ed. (Cambridge: Univ. Press, 1996). Elizabeth Faue, *Community of Suffering & Struggle: Women, Men, and the Labor Movement in Minneapolis, 1915-1945* (Chapel Hill: University of North Carolina, 1991).

[18] Irons, 7.

[19] Kelley, 68-69.

[20] Daniel, 37.

[21] Irons, 45-46.

[22] Daniel, 38.

[23] Salmond, 6, 27.

[24] Salmond 27-28

[25] Irons, 57

[26] Salmond, 30.

[27] Irons, 58-59.

[28] Irons, 61.

[29] Daniel, 22.

[30] Salmond, 30.

[31] Bernstein, 302.

[32] Irons, 74.

[33] Daniel, 38.

[34] Salmond, 31.

[35] Daniel, 42.

[36] Irons, 69.

[37] Irons, 65.

[38] Irons, 76. Salmond, 32.

[39] Salmond, 39.

[40] Bernstein 305.

[41] Salmond, 39.

[42] Bernstein, 305.

[43] Salmond, 40.

[44] Salmond, 42.

[45] "Cotton Textile Strike Is Voted," *The Providence Journal*, August 17, 1934.

[46] Ibid.

[47] Salmond, 43.

[48] *The Providence Journal*, August 17, 1934.

[49] Ibid.

[50] Ibid.

[51] Ibid.

[52] Scott Molloy Research Collection 1864-2009(bulk 1864-2009).

[53] "Textile Leader Will Set Up Headquarters," *The Providence Journal*, August 21, 1934.

[54] "U.T.W. Council to Meet Here Saturday Afternoon," *The Providence Journal*, August 22, 1934.

[55] "R.I. Operatives Will Act Tomorrow On Decision Of Textile Unions To Strike," *The Woonsocket Call*, August 18, 1934.

[56] "Green Declares Strike Justified," *The Providence Journal*, August 30, 1934.

[57] "Wool Unions Get Walkout Order," *The Providence Journal*, September 1, 1934.

[58] Daniel, *Culture of Misfortune*, 23-24.

[59] Jennifer Luff, *Commonsense Anticommunism: Labor and Civil Liberties between the World Wars* (Chapel Hill: The University of North Carolina Press, 2012), 150.

[60] C. A. Hathaway, *Communists in the Textile Strike: An Answer to Gorman, Green and Co.* (New York, New York: Central Committee of the Communist Party U.S.A., 1934), 14.

[61] Ibid.

[62] "Cotton Textile Strike Called for Tomorrow Night; 11th Hour Conference is Failure," *The Providence Journal*, August 31, 1934.

[63] Ibid.

[64] Ibid.

[65] The Board Garrison led was called the National Labor Relations Board, but it should not be confused with the National Labor Relations Board created by the Wagner Act of 1935. The website of the current NLRB refers to Garrison's board as "the old NLRB." https://www.nlrb.gov/about-nlrb/who-we-are/our-history/1933-the-nlb-and-the-old-nlrb

[66] Ibid.

[67] Ibid.

[68] "Organizer Denies Sept. 4 Date Set," *The Providence Journal*, August 27, 1934.

[69] "Joseph Sylvia Hurt in Motor Accident," *The Providence Journal*, August 29, 1934.

[70] "Strike Leader Announces Plan to Picket Mills," *The Providence Journal*, September 1, 1934.

[71] Ibid.

[72] "Employers Say Few Will Strike," *The Providence Journal*, September 1, 1934.

[73] "Strike Leader Announces Plan to Picket Mills," *The Providence Evening Bulletin*, September 1, 1934.

[74] Ibid.

[75] Ibid.

[76] Ibid.

[77] "Sloan Calls Union Demands Preposterous and Ruinous," *The Providence Journal*, September 2, 1934.

[78] Gary Gerstle, *Working-Class Americanism: The Politics of Labor in a Textile City, 1914-1960* (Princeton and Oxford: Princeton University Press, 2002).

[79] "Most Employers in State Assert Few Will Strike," *The Providence Journal*, September 2, 1934.

[80] "Leader Says Strike to Go on In Spite Of 'Hell, High Water," *The Providence Journal*, September 4, 1934.

[81] Ibid.

[82] Ibid.

[83] Ibid.

[84] "Green Asks All to Remain Calm," *The Providence Journal*, September 9, 1934.

[85] Ibid.

[86] "Troy and Bodwell Clash Over Strike," *The Providence Journal*, September 8, 1934.

[87] "State Troopers Rout Mob of 2000 Strikers After Disorder at Saylesville Plant," *The Providence Journal* (Providence, Rhode Island), September 8, 1934.

[88] Ibid.

[89] Ibid.

[90] Sayles Finishing Plants (Saylesville, Phillipsdale, and Valley Falls, Rhode Island, and Asheville, North Carolina) Business Records 1906 - 1971, The Sayles Finishing Plant Ephemera collection (MSS 6, sg 35), *Rhode Island Historical Society, Manuscripts Division*, Providence, Rhode Island. Hereafter referred to as *RIHS Strike Scrapbook*.

[91] "Riot at Saylesville, RI, As Night Shift Leaves," *The Boston Daily Globe*, September 8, 1934.

[92] "State Troopers Rout Mob of 2000 Strikers After Disorder at Saylesville Plant," *The Providence Journal*, September 8, 1934.

[93] Ibid.

[94] Ibid.

[95] Ibid.

[96] Ibid.

[97] "Woonsocket Men Vote to Strike," *The Providence Journal*, September 9, 1934.

[98] Ibid.

[99] Ibid. Schmetz's union would itself become embroiled in violence the following week, and while the events in Woonsocket are not the focus of this paper, are a subject worthy of deeper analysis in themselves.

[100] "Police Act to Stop Intimidation of Mill Workers in Providence," *The Providence Journal* (Providence, Rhode Island), September 10, 1934.

[101] "1500 at Strike Meeting in Pawtuxet Valley," *The Providence Journal* (Providence, Rhode Island), September 10, 1934.

[102] Erwin L. Levine, *Theodore Francis Green: The Rhode Island Years, 1906-1936* (Providence, Rhode Island: Brown University Press, 1963), 1-10.

[103] Ibid., 139.

[104] "Governor Issues Call on Appeal of High Sheriff," *The Providence Journal*, September 11, 1934.

[105] "R.I. Mills Renew Resistance Today," *The Providence Journal*, September 10, 1934.

[106] *RIHS Strike Scrapbook*

[107] "R.I. Mills Renew Resistance Today," *The Providence Journal*, September 10, 1934.

[108] "Saylesville Armed Camp," *The Boston Daily Globe*, September 11, 1934.

[109] Ibid.

[110] James F. Findlay, "The Great Textile Strike of 1934: Illuminating Rhode Island History in the Thirties," *Rhode Island History* 42, no. 1 (Feb 1, 1983), 17.

[111] Ibid.

[112] Ibid.

[113] "16,000 Workers Out of Plants In Rhode Island," *The Providence Journal*, September 6, 1934.

[114] Findlay, 23.

[115] "Coats Employes (sic) Call on Governor to Protect Them," *The Providence Journal*, September 12, 1934.

[116] Ibid.

[117] "Green Orders Guardsmen Mobilized for Strike Duty; 3 Shot at Saylesville," *The Providence Journal*, September 11, 1934.

[118] Ibid.

[119] Ibid.

[120] "Saylesville Armed Camp," *The Boston Daily Globe*, September 11, 1934.

[121] "Green Orders Guardsmen Mobilized for Strike Duty; 3 Shot at Saylesville," *The Providence Journal*, September 11, 1934.

[122] Ibid.

[123] Ibid.

[124] Ibid.

[125] William Gerald MacLoughlin, *Rhode Island: A History* (New York, New York: W.W. Norton & Company, 1978). Erwin L. Levine, *Theodore Francis Green: The Rhode Island Years, 1906-1936* (Providence, Rhode Island: Brown University Press, 1963). McLoughlin's book is the only source to make mention of this Klan activity in Rhode Island during the strike but he offers no source for the claim.

[126] Salmond, 93.

[127] "Green Orders Guardsmen Mobilized for Strike Duty; 3 Shot at Saylesville," *The Providence Journal*, September 11, 1934.

[128] Ibid.

[129] *RIHS Scrapbook*

[130] "Bayonets Hold Back Sayles Plant Mobs," *The Providence Journal*, September 12, 1934.

[131] Ibid.

[132] "Strike Sidelights," *The Pawtucket Times*, September 13, 1934. And "Bayonets Hold Back Sayles Plant Mobs," *The Providence Journal*, September 12, 1934.

[133] "Bayonets Hold Back Sayles Plant Mobs," *The Providence Journal*, September 12, 1934.

[134] Ibid.

[135] Ibid.

[136] Ibid.

[137] Ibid.

[138] *Brown Alumni Monthly*, Vol. XXV, No. 4, (Providence, Rhode Island), November 1934.

[139] "Bayonets Hold Back Sayles Plant Mobs," *The Providence Journal* (Providence, Rhode Island), September 12, 1934.

[140] Ibid.

[141] Ibid.

[142] "Bayonets Hold Back Sayles Plant Mobs," *The Providence Journal*, September 12, 1934.

[143] "Strike Sidelights," *The Pawtucket Times*, September 12, 1934.

[144] "Bayonets Hold Back Sayles Plant Mobs," *The Providence Journal* (Providence,

Rhode Island), September 12, 1934.

[145] Ibid.

[146] Ibid.

[147] "Strike Sidelights," *The Pawtucket Times*, September 12, 1934.

[148] "Bayonets Hold Back Sayles Plant Mobs," *The Providence Journal*, September 12, 1934.

[149] Erwin L. Levine, *Theodore Francis Green: The Rhode Island Years, 1906-1936* (Providence, Rhode Island: Brown University Press, 1963), 170.

[150] Ibid.

[151] Ibid.

[152] Robert B. Dresser, "The Case for Tax Relief", *The Freeman* (Orange, Connecticut), Vol. 5, No. 3, September 1954. Robert B. Dresser, "Statement of Robert B. Dresser," *Committee for Constitutional Government* (New York, New York), undated. https://history.fee.org/publications/statement-of-robert-b-dresser/

[153] *Survey Report African American Struggle for Civil Rights in Rhode Island: The Twentieth Century*, RI Historical Preservation and Heritage Commission (Providence, Rhode Island), July 2, 2019.
http://www.preservation.ri.gov/pdfs_zips_downloads/
resources_pdfs/2019twentiethc_ri_afam-civil-rights_report.pdf

[154] "Robert B. Dresser, Lawyer and Conservative Spokesman," The *New York Times*, September 26, 1976.

[155] "Bayonets Hold Back Sayles Plant Mobs," *The Providence Journal*, September 12, 1934.

[156] "Three of Mob Dying in Sayles Mill Riot," *The Providence Journal*, September 13, 1934.

[157] "2 Badly Wounded by Trapped Troops in Cemetery Area," *The Pawtucket Times*, September 12, 1934.

[158] "Three of Mob Dying in Sayles Mill Riot," *The Providence Journal* (Providence, Rhode Island), September 13, 1934.

[159] "Soldiers, Driven Back by Rocks, Fire and Charge with Fixed Bayonets," *The Providence Evening Bulletin* (Providence, Rhode Island), September 12, 1934.

[160] Transcript of Interview with Harold Fletcher, *Mill Life Oral History Collection*, Box 25 ed., Vol. folder 36 (South Kingstown, Rhode Island: University of Rhode Island, 1974).

[161] "Soldiers, Driven Back by Rocks, Fire and Charge with Fixed Bayonets," *The Providence Evening Bulletin* (Providence, Rhode Island), September 12, 1934.

[162] "Three of Mob Dying in Sayles Mill Riot," *The Providence Journal* (Providence, Rhode Island), September 13, 1934.

[163] Ibid.

[164] Ibid.

[165] Ibid.

[166] "Soldiers, Driven Back by Rocks, Fire and Charge with Fixed Bayonets," *The Providence Journal*, September 12, 1934.

[167] Ibid. Fletcher Oral History.

[168] "2 Badly Wounded By Trapped Troops In Cemetery Area," *The Pawtucket Times*, September 12, 1934.

[169] "Three of Mob Dying in Sayles Mill Riot," *The Providence Journal*, September 13, 1934.

[170] Ibid.

[171] "Soldiers, Driven Back by Rocks, Fire and Charge with Fixed Bayonets," *The Providence Journal*, September 12, 1934.

[172] "Three of Mob Dying in Sayles Mill Riot," *The Providence Journal*, September 13, 1934.

[173] Ibid.

[174] Ibid.

[175] "Rhode Island Governor Issues Proclamation," *The New York Times* (New York, NY), September 13, 1934.

[176] "Three of Mob Dying in Sayles Mill Riot," *The Providence Journal*, September 13, 1934.

[177] Ibid.

[178] Ibid.

[179] Ibid.

[180] Ibid.

[181] "Quiet Prevails in Strike Area," *The Providence Journal*, September 14, 1934.

[182] Ibid.

[183] "None of Green's Plan to Meet Crisis Adopted," *The Providence Journal* (Providence, Rhode Island), September 14, 1934.

[184] Ibid.

[185] Ibid.

[186] Ibid.

[187] *RIHS Strike Scrapbook*

[188] "None of Green's Plan to Meet Crisis Adopted," *The Providence Journal*, September 14, 1934.

[189] Ibid.

[190] Ibid.

[191] For an interesting look at McCoy, please review Mathew J. Smith's "The Real McCoy," *Rhode Island History* (Providence, Rhode Island), Vol. 32, Number 3, August 1973. Smith is a former Rhode Island Speaker of the House of Representatives.

[192] "None of Green's Plan to Meet Crisis Adopted," *The Providence Journal*, September 14, 1934.

[193] Ibid.

[194] Ibid.

[195] Ibid.

[196] "Green's Strike Program Killed by Adjournment," *The Providence Journal*, September 15, 1934.

[197] Ibid.

[198] Clipping from, *The Pawtucket Times*, September 14, 1934, found in *RIHS Strike Scrapbook*.

[199] "15 Communists Arrested in Drive Throughout City," *The Providence Journal*, September 14, 1934.

[200] "Subversive Radical Influence Is Evident in State, Police Say," *The Providence Journal*, September 13, 1934.

[201] Ibid.

[202] "15 Communists Arrested in Drive Throughout City," *The Providence Journal*, September 14, 1934.

[203] Ibid.

[204] "Labor Defense Demands Impeachment of Green," *The Providence Journal*, September 16, 1934.

[205] "8 Alleged 'Reds' Appear on Trial," *The Providence Journal* (Providence, Rhode Island), October 3, 1934.

[206] "Finishing Plant at Saylesville to Reopen Today," *The Providence Journal*, September 19, 1934.

[207] "1100 Employes (sic) Return to Jobs at Saylesville," *The Providence Journal*, September 20, 1934.

[208] Salmond, 52-54.

[209] "Winant Board Asks for End of Strike with Jobs Assured," *The New York Times*, September 21, 1934.

[210] Salmond, 76.

[211] "Roosevelt Approves Winant Body Plan," *The Providence Journal*, September 21, 1934.

[212] "Winant Board Asks for End of Strike with Jobs Assured," *The New York Times*, September 21, 1934.

[213] Ibid.

[214] Ibid.

[215] "Mill Hands Ordered to Return Tomorrow," *The Providence Journal*, September 23, 1934.

[216] Salmond, 78.

[217] *RIHS Strike Scrapbook.*

[218] "A.F.L. Resolution Scores Governor," *The Providence Journal*, October 7, 1934.

[219] Ibid.

[220] "R.I. Labor Refuses to Rebuke Green," *The Providence Journal*, October 8, 1934.

[221] "Labor Branch Blocks Rebuke to Governor," *The Newport Daily News*, October 8, 1934.

[222] "R.I. Labor Refuses to Rebuke Green," *The Providence Journal*, October 8, 1934.

[223] "Rites Thursday for Strike Victim," *The Providence Journal*, October 9, 1934.

[224] Erwin L. Levine, *Theodore Francis Green: The Rhode Island Years, 1906-1936* (Providence, Rhode Island: Brown University Press, 1963).

[225] Mathew J. Smith, "The Real McCoy," *Rhode Island History* (Providence, Rhode Island), Vol. 32, Number 3, August 1973.

[226] Kelly, *Nine Lives For Labor*, 65-88.

[227] John Harris, "Roosevelt Pleased Troops Not Needed: Secretary Dern Reveals 4000 Held Ready," *The Daily Boston Globe*, September 16, 1934.

[228] Transcript of Interview with Rachel Landry, *Mill Life Oral History Collection*, box 27, folder 56 (South Kingstown, Rhode Island: University of Rhode Island, 1974).

[229] ""Just having Fun" Arrested Rioters Declare." *The Indiana Gazette*, September 13, 1934. https://www.newspapers.com/clip/282616/the_indiana_gazette/.

[230] "Many Pawtucket Society Folk Enjoying Southern Sojourns," *The Providence Sunday Journal*, February 3, 1935.

ABOUT THE AUTHOR

Patrick Crowley

Patrick Crowley currently serves as the Secretary-Treasurer of the Rhode Island AFL-CIO. He was worked as a union organizer in both Massachusetts and Rhode Island since 1996. Patrick earned a bachelor's degree in Philosophy from Bridgewater State College, a master's degree in Labor Studies from the University of Massachusetts Amherst, and a  master's degree in History from the University of Rhode Island.

He is also the author of the journal article "African-American Led Worker Solidarity in World War Two Providence," published in the Fall 2021 edition of Rhode Island History: The Journal of the Rhode Island Historical Society.